THE PHILOSOPHY OF TOLKIEN

PETER KREEFT

THE
PHILOSOPHY
OF
TOLKIEN

THE WORLDVIEW BEHIND
The Lord of the Rings

IGNATIUS PRESS   SAN FRANCISCO

ACKNOWLEDGMENTS

Excerpts from the works of C. S. Lewis
are copyright © by C. S. Lewis Pte., Ltd., and are used by permission.

Excerpts from the works of J. R. R. Tolkien
are reprinted by permission of HarperCollins Publishers, Ltd.

Specific C. S. Lewis books for which Harcourt, Inc., has also granted permission for excerpts:

Letters to Malcolm: Chiefly on Prayer, copyright © 1964, 1963 by C. S. Lewis Pte., Ltd. and renewed 1992, 1991 by Arthur Owen Barfield.

The Four Loves, copyright © 1960 by C. S. Lewis and renewed 1988 by Arthur Owen Barfield.

Poems, copyright © 1964 by the Executors of the Estate of C. S. Lewis and renewed 1992 by C.S. Lewis Pte., Ltd.

Surprised by Joy: The Shape of My Early Life, copyright © 1956 by C. S. Lewis and renewed 1984 by Arthur Owen Barfield.

Specific J. R. R. Tolkien books for which HarperCollins Publishers, Ltd., has also granted permission for excerpts:

The Silmarillion, copyright © 1977 by J. R. R. Tolkien.

"On Fairy-Stories", copyright © 1947, 1966 by J. R. R. Tolkien.

Letters of J. R. R. Tolkien, copyright © 1981 by George Allen & Unwin, Ltd.

The Fellowship of the Ring, copyright © 1954, 1965, 1966 by J. R. R. Tolkien, renewed 1993, 1994.

The Two Towers, copyright © 1954, 1965, 1966 by J. R. R. Tolkien, renewed 1993, 1994.

The Return of the King, copyright © 1955, 1965, 1966 by J. R. R. Tolkien, renewed 1993, 1994.

Cover photo: Corbis

Cover design by Riz Boncan Marsella

© 2005 Ignatius Press, San Francisco
All rights reserved
ISBN 978-1-58617-025-7
Library of Congress control number 20033115832
Printed in the United States of America ∞

CONTENTS

Introduction

Oh, no! Not *another* book on Tolkien!
Why should you read this one?

Most of us can remember where we were when certain tragic historical events occurred in America, such as 9/11, the Kennedy assassination, Pearl Harbor.

Most of us can also remember where we were when we first discovered *The Lord of the Rings*.

We remember the excitement of discovery. Here was a world that was *real*—in fact, more real, more solid than the one we left when we opened the covers of that book. Those covers were magic doors, and we really walked through them into Tolkien's world. They were not just windows to peer through, like cages at a zoo. We were not tourists but natives. We knew this world. It was our own world, seen more clearly than we had ever seen it before.

Exploring Tolkien's world was not just interesting (that all-purpose meaningless euphemism). It was not even just fascinating. It was sheer joy. For we knew that here we had touched truth. This book was a homecoming. This book broke our hearts.

Subsequent readings confirmed the reality and truth of Tolkien's world, and joy rose again like the sun. No one reads *The Lord of the Rings* only once; and that is the clearest mark of a Great Book.

But when we read secondary sources, books about *The Lord of the Rings*, we do not feel the same excitement of discovery, joy, and grateful wonder. We do not smell the same sharp smell of truth, even when these books tell the truth. For we do not want someone else to tell us what Tolkien told us. We do not want summaries of Tolkien, we want Tolkien. We do not want books about Tolkien's world, we want Tolkien's world.

This book is not about Tolkien's world. It is about Tolkien's worldview, Tolkien's philosophy. Exploring *that* can be another adventure. For while this philosophy is as much a part of Tolkien's world as its wars, its life forms, its history, its beauties, and its terrors, the philosophy is not on the surface, as are these other things, but hidden beneath it, or behind it, or inside it, inside the things and events in the story. If *The Lord of the Rings* were an allegory, the philosophy would be on the surface, like rocks. Instead, it is more like the molten core of the earth: central but hidden.

Therefore this book can be a second adventure of discovery. After you read it, you will know why you knew you had touched Truth when you first read *The Lord of the Rings*.

Four different uses of this book

This book is four types of book in one.

First, it is a good read, and a voyage of discovery into the philosophical heart of Middle-earth.

Second, it can be used as a research tool, a concordance. The philosophical themes in *The Lord of the Rings* are outlined and organized into fifty questions, accompanied by numerous references to the text of *The Lord of the Rings* and to the three works of Tolkien's that form the most authentic commentary on it: his essay "On Fairy-Stories", *The Silmarillion*, and *The Letters of J. R. R. Tolkien*. (See pages 229ff.)

Researching is much more exciting than rehashing. I still remember the excitement of first learning to use a concordance to study the Bible. I learned far more from that than from any secondary sources. A concordance is like a laboratory manual rather than a science textbook, or like a piece of sheet music rather than a prerecorded CD, or like a cookbook rather than a plate of leftovers. It is a road map for your own travels rather than a travel journal recounting someone else's.

Third, this book can be used as an engaging introduction to philosophy. For many of the great questions of philosophy are included in the fifty-question outline, but not dressed in suits of armor, not in rigid definitions and arguments abstracted from the field of battle.

If used in a philosophy class, I suggest using it in tandem with a classic novel or poem that represents the most completely opposite philosophy, such as Jean-Paul Sartre's *Nausea*, Albert Camus's *The Stranger*, Lucretius's *On the Nature of Things*, B. F. Skinner's *Walden Two*, William Faulkner's *The Sound and the Fury*, or Thomas Hardy's *The Dynasts*.

This book presents four tools for understanding each of the philosophical issues *The Lord of the Rings* treats:

a. an explanation of the meaning and importance of the question;

b. a key quotation from *The Lord of the Rings* showing how Tolkien answered the question (many more passages are given in the Concordance to *The Lord of the Rings* in the Appendix);

c. a quotation from Tolkien's other writings (usually a letter) that explains or comments on the theme in *The Lord of the Rings*;

d. a quotation from C. S. Lewis, Tolkien's closest friend, showing the same philosophy directly stated.

Because present-day writers are limited in the extent to which they may quote these writers, the reader will want to look up passages in their works that are referred to in this book. All Tolkien references are to the one-volume American edition (Boston: Houghton Mifflin, 1994) of *The Lord of the Rings* [LOTR].

The book can also be used to explore the very close parallel between Tolkien and Lewis. Most of the parallels are not due to direct influence, either way, but to a common familiarity with and respect for the same sources in the great tradition, that is, pre-modern Western literature, philosophy, and religion.

G. K. Chesterton and Hilaire Belloc were so close, in personal friendship, in philosophical and religious belief, and in the common vocation of fighting a common *jihad* against the modern world, that they were called "the Chesterbelloc monster". We could with equal reason speak of "the Tolkie-lewis monster".

But Tolkien wasn't a philosopher!

"The *philosophy* of Tolkien"? Isn't that like "the politics of Chopin" or "the theology of Euclid"? Tolkien was not a philosopher but a philologist.

True, Tolkien was not a professional philosopher—and probably neither are you. But he had a very distinctive and definite philosophy, a world-and-life-view (as the Germans say, a *Weltanschauung* and a *Lebensschauung*). And his philosophy could not possibly be excluded from his life's work. Like religion, sex, age, and race, philosophy permeates everything we do. A Hindu would have written a very different *Lord of the Rings* than a Catholic. A woman would have written a different *Lord of the Rings* than a man. A teenager would have written a different *Lord of the Rings* than an adult. An Italian would have written a very different *Lord of the Rings* than an Englishman. And it is equally certain that a Marxist, a Cartesian rationalist, a Hegelian Idealist, a Nietzschean nihilist, or (God help us!) a Derridadaist deconstructionist would have written a very different *Lord of the Rings* than Tolkien did. Philosophy is not confined to philosophers, thank God. Everyone has a philosophy. As Cicero famously said, you have no choice between having a philosophy and not having one, only between having a good one and having a bad one. And not to admit that you have a philosophy at all is to have a bad one. For it is one that does not know itself. So how could it know anything else, especially us?

The greatness of *The Lord of the Rings*

The literary establishment in England was stunned, shocked, and scandalized by an event of millennial significance when a major bookstore chain innocently polled English-speaking readers, asking them to choose the greatest book of the twentieth century. By a wide margin *The Lord of the Rings* won. Three times the poll was broadened: to a worldwide readership, into cyberspace via Amazon.com, and even to "the greatest book of the millennium". The same champion won each time.

The critics retched and kvetched, wailed and flailed, gasped and grasped for explanations. One said that they had failed and wasted their work of "ed-u-ca-tion". "Why bother teaching them to read if they're going to read *that*?"

The polls revealed one important thing about *The Lord of the Rings*: that it is a classic, that is, a book loved by humanity, by human nature, wherever it is found. And they revealed one important thing about the critics: that humanity isn't found in that arrogant oligarchy of utterly out-of-touch elitists. And they revealed one important thing about our culture, the same thing revealed by many polls that ask questions about values and about philosophy: that our culture is *not* egalitarian at all, in fact, that it is perhaps the least egalitarian culture in the history of the world. For in what other culture has the worldview and life view of the teachers differed so radically from that of the students?

Every human soul craves "the good, the true, and the beautiful" absolutely and without limit. And it is precisely about these three most fundamental values that the gap is the widest. Ordinary people still believe in a real morality, a real difference between good and evil; and in objective truth and the possibility of knowing it; and in the superiority of beauty over ugliness. But our educators, or "experts" (Fr. Richard John Neuhaus calls them "the chattering classes"), feel toward these three traditional values the way people think medieval inquisitors felt toward witches. Our artists deliberately prefer ugliness to beauty, our moralists fear goodness more than evil, and our philosophers embrace various forms of post-modernism that reduce truth to ideology or power.

So it is no surprise that in a culture in which philosophers scorn wisdom, moralists scorn morality, preachers are the world's greatest hypocrites, sociologists are the only people in the world who do not know what a good society is, psychologists have the most mixed-up psyches, professional artists are the only ones in the world who actually hate beauty, and liturgists are to religion what Dr. Von Helsing is to Dracula—it is no surprise that in this culture the literary critics are the last people to know a good book when they see one.

So, what should we do about it? Just ignore them. That will do more to save civilization than anything else you can possibly do (except becoming a saint). It will also make them very angry, for, like teenagers, the critics' greatest joy is to be shocking, and their greatest fear is to be ignored. *The Lord of the Rings* is a touchstone. W. H. Auden said, "If someone dislikes it, I shall never trust [his] literary judgment about anything again."[1] It is a touchstone for more than literary judgment; it is a touchstone for one's whole personality. Those who love Tolkien are almost always *good* people, honest people. Some are Hobbit-like and some are Elvish, but none are Orcish. Not all Tolkien haters are Orcs, but all Orcs are Tolkien haters.

But *why* did almost everyone else except the critics judge *The Lord of the Rings* the greatest book of the century? I have not found a better answer to that question than C. S. Lewis's review of the first volume:

> Nothing quite like it was ever done before. . . . Probably no book yet written in the world is quite such a radical instance of what its author has else where called "sub-creation." . . . Not content to create his own story, he creates, with an almost insolent prodigality, the whole world in which it is to move, with its own theology, myths, geography, history, paleography, languages, and orders of beings—a world "full of strange creatures beyond count." The names alone are a feast. . . . You can hardly put your foot down anywhere . . . without stirring the dust of history. Our own world, except at certain rare moments, hardly seems too heavy with its past. . . . This is surely the utmost reach of invention, when an author produces what seems to be not even his own, much less anyone else's. Is mythopoeia, after all, not the most, but the least, subjective of activities?

[1] BBC programme *The Critics*, November 16, 1955.

This book is like lightning from a clear sky . . . here are beauties which pierce like swords or burn like cold iron; here is a book that will break your heart. It is a master key; use it on what door you like. . . . As for escapism, what we chiefly escape is the illusions of our ordinary life. "But why," (some ask) "why, if you have a serious comment to make on this real life of men, must you do it by [myth]?" Because, I take it, one of the main things the author wants to say is that the real life of men is of that mythical and heroic quality. . . . The value of the myth is that it takes all the things we know and restores to them the rich significance which had been hidden by "the veil of familiarity." The child enjoys his cold meat (otherwise dull to him) by pretending it is buffalo, just killed with his own bow and arrow. And the child is wise. The real meat comes back to him more savoury for having been dipped in a story; you might say that only then is it the real meat. If you are tired of the real landscape, look at it in a mirror. By putting bread, gold, horse, apple, or the very roads into a myth, we do not retreat from reality: we rediscover it. As long as the story lingers in our mind, the real things are more themselves. This book applies the treatment not only to bread or apple but to good and evil, to our endless perils, our anguish, and our joys. By dipping them in myth we see them more clearly.

This book is too original and too opulent for any final judgment. . . . But we know at once that it has done things to us. We are not quite the same men.[2]

The Lord of the Rings heals our culture as well as our souls. It gives us the most rare and precious thing in modern literature: the heroic. It is a call to heroism; it is a horn like

[2] C. S. Lewis, in *Time and Tide*, August 14, 1954, and October 22, 1955. Reprinted in Lesley Walmsley, ed., *C. S. Lewis: Essay Collection and Other Short Pieces* (London: HarperCollins, 2000).

the horn of Rohan, which Merry received from Theoden and used to rouse the Hobbits of the Shire from their sheepish niceness and passivity to throw off their tyrants, first in their souls and then in their society. The deepest healing is the healing of the deepest wound. The deepest wound is the frustration of the deepest need. The deepest need is the need for meaning, purpose, and hope. And that is what *The Lord of the Rings* offers us. As C. S. Lewis said, "The most obvious appeal of the book is perhaps also its deepest: 'there was sorrow then too, and gathering dark, but great valour, and great deeds that were not wholly vain.' *Not wholly vain*—it is the cool middle point between illusion and disillusionment." [3]

Clyde Kilby tells us that "someone wrote me of a sixth-grade pupil who, after reading *The Lord of the Rings*, had cried for two days. I think it must have been a cry for life and meaning and joy from the wasteland." [4]

How its philosophy makes it great

Every story, long or short, has five dimensions. They are usually called its (1) plot, (2) characters, (3) setting, (4) style, and (5) theme. We could call them, respectively, the story's (1) work, (2) workers, (3) world, (4) words, and (5) wisdom. "Philosophy" means "the love of wisdom". So a story's philosophy is one of its five basic dimensions.

Which "dimension" sold *The Lord of the Rings*? All five. To be great, a work of art must be great in not just one dimension but all, just as a healthy body needs to be healthy in all its

[3] Ibid.
[4] Clyde Kilby, *Tolkien and the Silmarillion* (Wheaton, Ill.: Harold Shaw Publishers, 1976), p. 79.

organs, a healthy soul in all its powers (mind, will, and emotions), and a morally good act in all its dimensions (the deed, the motive, and the circumstances).

A great story must have, first of all, a good plot, a great deed, a good work, something worth doing. You cannot write a great story about saving a button on a sweater and nothing more. You can, however, write a great story about saving the world, which is what Tolkien did.

Second, a great story must also have great characters or at least one great character (greatly drawn, at least) for readers to identify with, to find their identity in. We *become* the characters—in spirit, in imagination. No story is great unless it sucks us in, takes us up out of our bodies, and gives us an out-of-body experience, an *ek-stasis*, standing outside yourself in another. Great stories give us the grace of a mystical experience, on the level of the imagination.

Nearly all of Tolkien's characters are identifiable-with, even Ents. Who would have believed that any author could conjure up, in adult human beings, literary belief in *talking trees*? And Hobbits: What other author has ever successfully created a whole new *species*? And who else has ever given us more credible Elves? We *know* these are the real Elves; we must have an innate Elf detector, an innate Jungian archetype of true Elvishness. Even inanimate things—forests, horns, swords—are characters with memorable, credible personalities.

Third, a great story also should have a great setting, an interesting world. Sometimes it is a familiar part of this world, sometimes an unfamiliar part of this world, and sometimes another world. *The Lord of the Rings'* setting is *not* another world, but a historically unfamiliar portion of this world: its mythical past. "Middle-earth" is an old name for "the third rock from the sun".

Sometimes, the setting is at a minimum (e.g., in *The Three Musketeers*: the book, not the movie). Sometimes, it is at a maximum, when the setting is the most memorable dimension of all (e.g., *City of Joy*: again, the book, not the movie; or Hal Clement's sci-fi classic *Mission of Gravity*). The importance of the setting varies with the genre. It is the most in epic and the least in drama.

Many readers find the setting of *The Lord of the Rings*—Middle-earth itself—to be its most captivating aspect. In America, legally, and also in Kazakhstan, illegally, people come together to stage day-long outdoor reenactments of the plot, using many acres of land, many characters in costumes (usually playing multiple roles), weapons, battles, etc. This has never been done for *Death of a Salesman*.

What of the fourth dimension, style? Sometimes a great story is told in a plain style (e.g., the Koiné Greek of Mark's Gospel), or even a bad style (e.g., the fairy tales of George MacDonald). A great style can sometimes make up for a small story (Sartre, Samuel Beckett, Ernest Hemingway, John Gardner, James Stephens), but more often a bad style ruins a good story (Thomas Wolfe, Olaf Stapleton, David Lindsay, even George MacDonald).

Even his most severe critics admit Tolkien's excellence in one aspect of style: language, especially his proper names. Tolkien tells us that the whole of *The Lord of the Rings* emerged from this preoccupation (*The Lord of the Rings*, Introduction, p. xv).[5]

But surely the most valuable of all the gifts a story can give us is its fifth dimension: its wisdom, its philosophy, its world-and-life-view, its insight into ourselves and our lives and our

---

[5] All references are to the one-volume, American edition (Boston: Houghton Mifflin, 1994) of *The Lord of the Rings* (hereafter cited as LOTR).

world. Stories do not do this directly and deliberately (as preaching does) or abstractly (as philosophy does), but they do it. It is therefore perfectly proper to explore this crucial dimension, this depth dimension of *The Lord of the Rings*, especially if *The Lord of the Rings* is "the greatest book of the century" and this is, in some ways, the greatest dimension of a book.

But it is only one dimension. This book is not about *The Lord of the Rings* but only its philosophy. It therefore leaves out far more than it leaves in. Any good book about a classic must do that, or it would be a classic itself. I leave out such wonderful things as the fascinating yet familiar characters, the elaborate yet satisfying plot, the realistic yet fantastic setting, the simple yet archaic writing style, the historical revolution wrought by *The Lord of the Rings* in the field of fantasy and in our society's attitude toward it, and much, much more. *The Lord of the Rings* is a deep mine with many precious gems, deep enough for many others to plumb to their hearts' content. But I am a philosopher, and the search for wisdom is my quest.

Though Tolkien's philosophy can be gleaned from the story, the story is not simply a vessel for philosophy. A true work of art, as opposed to a work of propaganda, never is. But as a fruit of the imagination, *The Lord of the Rings* is infused with the same light that illumined the man who wrote it. And that light is true, for it reveals the reality of the world and life. And it is also *good*, because it heals our blindness. Like the Fellowship itself, Tolkien's philosophy fights. It conquers what George Orwell called the "smelly little orthodoxies" of political correctness that have twisted and wounded our souls. In other words, it is like the healing herb *athelas* (see LOTR, p. 193).

The relation between philosophy and literature

Philosophy and literature belong together. They can work
like the two lenses of a pair of binoculars. Philosophy argues
abstractly. Literature argues too—it persuades, it changes the
reader—but concretely. Philosophy says truth, literature
shows truth.

For instance, a philosopher like Hegel may argue that each
individual is somehow responsible for all because society is a
natural and organic whole, a "concrete universal" with "internal relations". In *The Brothers Karamazov*, however, Fyodor
Dostoyevski not only has one of his characters (Father
Zossima) *say* this ("We are each responsible for all") but also
has all the characters, both good and evil, *show* it, live it,
exemplify it. Sartre argues philosophically that life is "absurd"
in his brilliant but unreadable *Being and Nothingness*, but he
shows it dramatically in the novel *Nausea* and plays such as
No Exit.

God must have known that literature is a more effective
teacher than philosophy, for when He chose to teach man-
kind its most important theological and moral lessons, He did
so not primarily through abstract eternal truths but through
historical events, through acts. The Bible is primarily literature, not philosophy; concrete, not abstract; narrative, not
explanation. Its wisdom literature, or philosophical books, are
commentary on its historical books, in both Testaments.

Human thought is both concrete (particular) and abstract
(universal) at the same time. We cannot think of abstract
universals like "man" without imagining some concrete, particular example of a man. Whenever we think of an abstract
universal, we have to use a particular concrete image. But the
converse is also true: whenever we recognize a concrete

particular as intelligible and meaningful, we use an abstract universal to classify it, to categorize it, to define it: we see or imagine Joe as a man, not an ape. Unless, of course, we are "educated" enough to treat abstractions as realities and join the ranks of "the chattering classes", who can actually believe absurdities like duties to abstractions like "humanity". But you need a Ph.D. to do that.

When you look through binoculars, you look through both lenses at once. Because human thought is binocular, abstract philosophy and concrete literature naturally reinforce each other's vision. Philosophy makes literature clear, literature makes philosophy real. Philosophy shows essences, literature shows existence. Philosophy shows meaning, literature shows life.

Allegory

It is not right to say that all literature illustrates a philosophy. The form of literature that illustrates philosophy is allegory. In an allegory each concrete thing *means* an abstract concept. In *The Pilgrim's Progress*, the pilgrim is simply Everyman as pilgrim, and the giant Despair is simply despair. Tolkien was not an allegorist, except once, in "Leaf by Niggle". He said, "I cordially dislike allegory in all its manifestations, and always have done so since I grew old enough to detect its presence" (LOTR, p. xvii).

Literature incarnates philosophy. You actually *see* fate when you read *Oedipus Rex*. You actually *hear* nihilism when you read *Waiting for Godot*. As the acts of the body *are* the acts of the person, as a smile does not merely *express* happiness (the nine-letter word does that) but actually *contains* it, so literature actually contains or incarnates philosophical truths (or falsehoods).

All literature incarnates some philosophy. Thus all literature teaches. In allegory, the philosophy is taught by the conscious and calculating part of the mind, while in great literature it is done by the unconscious and contemplative part of the mind, which is deeper and wiser and has more power to persuade and move the reader. Allegory engages only the mind, while great literature engages the whole person; for allegory comes from only the mind, while great literature comes from the whole person.

Literature not only incarnates a philosophy; it also tests it by verifying or falsifying it. One way literature tests philosophy is by putting different philosophies into the laboratory of life, incarnating them in different characters and then seeing what happens. Life does exactly the same thing. Literature also tests philosophy in a more fundamental way. It can be expressed by this rule: a philosophy that cannot be translated into a good story cannot be a good philosophy.

For instance, determinism, the philosophy that denies free will for the sake of fate, is shown to be a bad philosophy by pitiful literary efforts to incarnate it, like Skinner's *Walden Two*, and even by great but impossible efforts, like Hardy's *The Dynasts*. But the mysterious interplay of fate and free will is the stuff of all great literature (e.g., Leo Tolstoy's *War and Peace* and, of course, *The Lord of the Rings* itself). The opposite philosophical error of existentialist nihilism, which denies all fate or destiny and even purpose for the sake of freedom, also has never been able to produce a great story. It can, however, produce emotionally engaging ones, such as Camus's books *The Stranger* and *The Plague*.

Actually, that is not quite accurate. I would argue that Camus implicitly writes from a point of view that is on the way to theism. He at least wishes and perhaps even hopes that there is a God, an Author, and thus a meaning and a destiny to human life, even while he does not believe it—like his heroic protagonist Dr. Rieux in *The Plague*, who lives and gives like a saint, yet does not believe in God, and wonders how one can be a saint without God. A convinced and settled atheist like Sartre would never take God seriously enough to invent a Dr. Rieux—or, certainly, to *be* a person like Dr. Rieux.

The philosophy is in the point of view, and the point of view lies not in the picture but in the frame. For example, a theistic frame, or point of view, is present in Shakespeare's *Macbeth* and is deliberately removed in Faulkner's *The Sound and the Fury* (the title refers to Macbeth's great "Tomorrow" speech). Faulkner shows us what the world and life look like from the point of view of Macbeth himself, a morally insane soul on his way to Hell. But when we read Shakespeare we *judge* Macbeth to be insane from an implicitly higher point of view, which "frames" the portrait of Macbeth.

Literature is judgmental. It could not be philosophical if it were not. Even when it is nonjudgmental, it is judgmental, for nonjudgmentalism judges against all judgmental systems. For instance, we judge Faust to be a wicked, damned fool in Christopher Marlowe's version of the play, but *not* in Goethe's, for Goethe does not believe the frame, which is Christianity. In Goethe the opposite judgment is made: that Faust is a complete man, integrating his light and dark sides, his God and his devil, by learning and growing from every experience, even those experiences Catholics call mortal sins. His Nietzschean "beyond good and evil" does not judge against evil, but it does judge against something: against the Christian "judgmentalism", against the moral dualism that judges against evil.

In an allegory, the philosophical frame becomes the story. The plot and the characters are there only for that reason:

they are used as means to illustrate the philosophy. That is why we do not love the characters or care about them much as individuals. They are lost in their archetypes. In non-allegorical stories, the philosophy serves the story, as a frame serves a picture; in allegory it is vice versa. Thus in non-allegory the story can test the philosophy, since the story has priority, as data have priority over theory in science.

I know *The Lord of the Rings* is not an allegory because I don't find myself saying, of anything in it, "That reminds me of this or that", but I constantly find myself saying, of this or that, "That reminds me of something in *The Lord of the Rings*." In fact, almost everything reminds me of something in *The Lord of the Rings*.

The philosophical themes

In outlining the themes, or kinds of questions, or basic divisions of philosophy, I move from the more abstract and theoretical questions (e.g., those of metaphysics and theology) to the more concrete and practical ones (e.g., those of personal ethics), even though this means beginning with the least *interesting* points to most readers. But these are the most philosophically *important* points; for ethics depends on metaphysics, and to see this logical dependence is itself one of the most important, and forgotten, lessons we need to learn today. We can fully understand concrete and specific tactics in a war, or in a game like chess or football, only when we understand the abstract and general principles of strategy. We can understand the motions of the planets only after first learning the principles of geometry, and we can understand a philosopher's ethics only after we understand his metaphysics, his worldview.

Of course, when we begin to *learn* about these things we all do so inductively: we begin not with general principles but with the concrete observation of the movements of the soldiers, chess pieces, football players, or planets. But when we *teach* them, it is a great time-saving device to teach deductively, to begin with general principles. The logical order of teaching any subject is often the reverse of the way we first learned it.

If this book were a work of literature, the logical order would destroy the story, the suspense. (Angels, who begin with general principles and know everything else by deduction from them, do not write stories.) But the purpose of this book is only to teach, not to fascinate, engage, amaze, or move the reader, as Tolkien does in *The Lord of the Rings*. I presuppose that you have already been swept away by "the great grey ineluctable wave" of *The Lord of the Rings*. This book is not like surfing but oceanography.

The philosophical questions are about:

1. metaphysics ("all-that-is", "worldview", "the big picture");
2. philosophical theology (God);
3. angelology (angels);
4. cosmology (the cosmos);
5. anthropology (man);
6. epistemology (knowledge);
7. philosophy of history;
8. aesthetics (beauty);
9. linguistics (philosophy of language);
10. political philosophy; and
11. ethics, which includes questions such as: *Is evil real? Are moral principles absolute? What is the greatest good? Why do we need the virtues of duty, courage, hope, obedience, honesty, friendship, humility, gift-giving, mercy, and charity?*

The fifty philosophical questions

Within these eleven areas of philosophy, *The Lord of the Rings* deals with fifty of the greatest questions that have been asked by the greatest minds in history. This list is far from a complete introduction to all the great questions of philosophy. But it is a representative sample of the most important of them, the ones that make the greatest difference in our lives.

1 METAPHYSICS
   1.1 How big is reality?
   1.2 Is the supernatural real?
   1.3 Are Platonic Ideas real?

2 PHILOSOPHICAL THEOLOGY
   2.1 Does God exist?
   2.2 Is life subject to divine providence?
   2.3 Are we both fated and free?
   2.4 Can we relate to God by "religion"?

3 ANGELOLOGY
   3.1 Are angels real?
   3.2 Do we have guardian angels?
   3.3 Could there be creatures between men and angels, such as Elves?

4 COSMOLOGY
   4.1 Is nature really beautiful?
   4.2 Do things have personalities?
   4.3 Is there real magic?

5 ANTHROPOLOGY
   5.1 Is death good or bad?
   5.2 Is romance more thrilling than sex?
   5.3 Why do humans have identity crises?
   5.4 What do we most deeply desire?

I

Metaphysics

Introduction

"Philosophy" means "the love of wisdom". It should be what it means. The fact that it has largely ceased to be that in modern "philosophy departments" does not mean that its essence has changed, but that its disciples have. Similarly, the fact that most Christians in North America are not martyrs or saints like the early Christians does not mean that the meaning of Christianity has changed, only that Christians have.

Metaphysics is the most important, most foundational, part of philosophy. It is rational, not irrational; it is a "science" in the broad, ancient sense of the word: a body of knowledge ordered through explanations and causes. Like the rest of philosophy, it does not use the modern scientific method. (Neither does anything else except modern science!) But it is a science, and it should not be classified under "the occult", as it is in some bookstores.

Unlike all other sciences, including other philosophical sciences, metaphysics explores reality as such, all of reality, not just some part or dimension of reality, such as living things, chemicals, human history, or morality. It seeks the truths, laws, and principles that are true of all being. ("Being" is the traditional term, but "reality" sounds more concrete and less occultic than "being".)

Here are a few sample questions of metaphysics:

— Is all being one, true, good, and beautiful?

— Is evil real?

— Is matter real?

— Is spirit real?

— Is God real?

— Is chance real?

— Is causality real?

— Is time real?

— How can a being change, that is, be both the same being it was, and also different?

— What is the relation between a thing's essence (*what* it is) and its existence (*that* it is)?

— Does language reflect reality? Are there in reality things (nouns), acts (verbs), qualities (adjectives), relations (prepositions and conjunctions), etc.?

— Are "universals" like justice, human nature, squareness, and redness real things, or real aspects of things, or only concepts, or only words?

The Lord of the Rings illuminates at least three important metaphysical questions:

1. How big is reality? Is it larger or smaller than our thought?

2. Does it include the supernatural?

3. Does it include universals, "Platonic Ideas", or "Jungian archetypes"?

1.1 How big is reality?

There are only three logically possible answers to this question.

The first is that "there are more things in heaven and earth (i.e., in reality) than are dreamed of in your philosophies (i.e., in thought)." That was Shakespeare's philosophy, as expressed by Hamlet to Horatio, who found it hard to believe in ghosts. This is the philosophy of the poet and of the happy man, for whom nature is a fullness, a moreness, and therefore wonderful. It is the philosophy of all pre-modern cultures.

The second possible answer is that there are *fewer* things in reality than in thought; that most of our thought is mere myth, error, convention, projection, fantasy, fallacy, folly, dream, etc. This is the philosophy of the unhappy man, the cynic, the pessimist: "Trust nobody and nothing." This philosophy is hardly ever found in any pre-modern culture, except in a small minority.

The third possibility is that there are exactly the same number of things in reality and in thought, that is, that we "know it all".

What difference does it make to your life which philosophy you believe?

It makes a total difference, a difference to absolutely every single thing in your life. It colors everything. For if you believe the first philosophy, as Shakespeare did, as Tolkien did, and as most pre-modern peoples did, then your fundamental attitude toward all reality is wonder and humility. You are like a small child in a large house. As Tolkien said in one of his letters, "You are inside a very great story." You expect mysteries, you expect moreness: terrors to stop your heart and joys to break it. Reality is *big*. I think of the simple, haunting line in Ingmar Bergman's movie *The Seventh Seal*: "It is the Angel of Death that's passing over us, Mia, it's the Angel of Death, the Angel of Death. *And he's very big.*" In this big world there may be not only things like dragons, but even heroes.

The larger-than-life world is the one our ancestors lived

in. Our culture's greatest sadness is that we no longer live in this world. Tolkien's greatest achievement is that he invites us to inhabit this world again. He shows us that this world is our home. He even shows us heroism: he not only shows us heroes but he also shows us that we ourselves believe in heroes. For after we have read Tolkien's unashamedly heroic epic, we do not say, "Well, that was a pleasant little escape from reality", but, "Hey! That was real!"

If you believe the second philosophy, that there are *fewer* things in Heaven and earth than are dreamed of in our philosophies, then you are cynical, skeptical, suspicious, bored, jaded, detached, ironic, and definitely non-heroic. You are a reductionist: you reduce mystery to puzzle, love to lust, thought to cybernetics, reasoning to rationalizing, ideals to desires, man to ape, God to myth. In other words, you are a typically modern or post-modern man. (Is there much of a difference?) You buy into the first step of the scientific method: "Doubt everything that is not proved; treat every thought as guilty until proved innocent, false until proved true." The older philosophy treated thoughts as we treat people in court: innocent until proved guilty. (Compare Socrates's method with Descartes's on this score.)

The third philosophy is rationalism, in fact, arrogant rationalism: Everything in my thought is real, and everything real is in my thought. In ancient Greece Parmenides said, "What is thought and what is real is the same", and in modern Germany Hegel said, "The real is the rational and the rational is the real"; but I think only those with a divinity complex can actually believe that. And even pantheists, who believe that the whole cosmos is only a thought or dream, believe it is not *our* dream but God's, and therefore still "more", or transcendent to our thought—unless there is some confusion between us (or me) and God, in which case a shrink or a smack will serve the soul better than a syllogism.

Thomas Howard calls good fantasy a "flight to reality" because, though its *details* are fictional, the nature of its world, its universal principles and values, are true. Tolkien shows us the nature of the real world by his fantasy. He is making a statement about reality, about being, about metaphysics when he says:

> The realm of fairy-story is wide and deep and high and filled with many things: all manner of beasts and birds are found there; shoreless seas and stars uncounted; beauty that is an enchantment, and an ever-present peril; both joy and sorrow as sharp as swords. In that realm a man may, perhaps, count himself fortunate to have wandered.[1]

The fundamental reason for the popularity of *The Lord of the Rings* is that people sense it is *real*. No mere *escape* from reality can be voted "the greatest book of the century".

And that is why Tolkien does not tell us half of what he knows about his world. You can tell everything about your fantasies, your dreams, or your thoughts, but not about anything real.

That is also why *The Lord of the Rings* bears endless rereading: it is heavy enough to bear the mind's journeys into it, like our world. In fact, it is perhaps the most "heavy", full, detailed, complex, *real* invented world in all of human literature.

Tolkien himself tells us that he felt, in creating it, as we feel in reading it: that it was discovered, not invented, that it had always been there, and it was as much a surprise to Tolkien to

---

[1] J. R. R. Tolkien, "On Fairy-Stories", in *The Tolkien Reader* (New York: Ballantine Books, 1966), p. 3.

discover it as it is to us: "I had the sense of recording what was already 'there,' somewhere; not of 'inventing.'" [2] Great authors often say that about the experience of writing their masterpieces.

C. S. Lewis wrote from the same point of view:

> We must not listen to [Alexander] Pope's maxim about the proper study of mankind. "Know then thyself, presume not God to scan,/ The proper study of mankind is man." The proper study of mankind is everything.
>
> We should never ask of anything "Is it real?" For everything is real. The proper question is, "A real *what*?" [3]

1.2 Is the supernatural real?

C. S. Lewis explains what supernaturalism means as clearly as anyone has ever done:

> Ever since men were able to think, they have been wondering about what this universe really is and how it came to be there. And, very roughly, two views have been held. First, there is what is called the materialist view. People who take that view think that matter and space just happen to exist, and always have existed, nobody knows why; and that the matter, behaving in certain fixed ways, has just happened, by a sort of fluke, to produce creatures like ourselves who are able to think. . . . The other view is the religious view. According to it, what is behind the universe is more like a mind than it is like anything else we know. That is to say, it is conscious, and has purposes, and

---

[2] *The Letters of J. R. R. Tolkien*, selected and edited by Humphrey Carpenter, with the assistance of Christopher Tolkien (Boston: Houghton Mifflin, 1981), p. 145. (Hereafter *Letters*.)

[3] C. S. Lewis, *Letters to Malcolm* (New York: Harcourt, Brace and World, 1963), p. 80.

prefers one thing to another. And on this view it made the universe . . . to produce creatures like itself—I mean, like itself to the extent of having minds.[4]

The supernatural is not the same as the magical. Magic can be part of nature. There is as much magic in *The Hobbit* as in *The Silmarillion*, but *The Hobbit* is not about the supernatural, while *The Silmarillion* is.

What difference does it make whether you are a naturalist or a supernaturalist? All the difference in the world. It makes a difference to everything. Imagine you are acting in a play. The supernaturalist is like one who believes that the play is not the whole of reality, that there is a far greater reality outside it. The naturalist denies that. Even though the supernaturalist and the naturalist may speak the same lines in the play, their meaning is not the same. Context makes a difference, and the supernatural is the ultimate context.

Tolkien, as a Christian, was of course a supernaturalist. As we shall see when we treat the topic of religion, Tolkien kept the supernatural hidden in *The Lord of the Rings*; yet it is ubiquitous, and he himself explicitly told us so.

Tolkien claims that fantasy naturally treats the supernatural:

> [F]airy-stories as a whole have three faces: the Mystical towards the Supernatural, the Magical towards Nature, and the Mirror of scorn and pity towards Man ("On Fairy-Stories", p. 26).

Fantasy treats the supernatural not because it is fantastic but because it is real.

C. S. Lewis gives the following "aesthetic" argument for supernaturalism in *Miracles*:

---

[4] C. S. Lewis, *Mere Christianity*, rev. ed. (New York: Macmillan, 1952), pp. 31–32.

As long as one is a Naturalist, "Nature" is only a word for "everything"—And Everything is not a subject about which anything very interesting can be said or (save by illusion) felt. . . . But everything becomes different when we recognize that Nature is a *creature*, a created thing, with its own particular tang or flavour. . . .

The Englishness of English is audible only to those who know some other language as well. In the same way and for the same reason, only Supernaturalists really see Nature. You must go a little away from her, and then turn round, and look back. Then at last the true landscape will become visible. You must have tasted, however briefly, the pure water from beyond the world before you can be distinctly conscious of the hot, salty tang of Nature's current.[5]

The capacity to evoke wonder, which is the great power of fantasy, almost *requires* supernaturalism. It is inconceivable that a worldly pragmatist like John Dewey or Karl Marx could write fantasy. Only a supernaturalistic metaphysics has room for it. It says that our world has edges, that it is not all there is, that there is more. In such a world you can never say, with the bored, jaded author of Ecclesiastes, "I have seen everything" (Eccles 1:14).

In Tolkien's *Silmarillion* the world is flat (until its fall) and therefore has an edge. A flat world is a physical symbol for a supernaturalistic metaphysics. It points to a "beyond" beyond its edges, a "more". But a round world is self-contained, and absolutely relative. In *The Silmarillion* the world is changed from flat to round as a divine punishment. This is far from fantastic; it is symbolically quite accurate. For, in fact, the divine punishment was that our worldview, rather than our world, was changed from supernaturalism to naturalism.

[5] C. S. Lewis, *Miracles* (New York: Macmillan Publishing, 1947, 1960), pp. 64–66.

Yet one edge, one absolute, remains even in our round, relative world, though not in space but in time. There is death, personal time's absolute edge (see section 5.1).

Supernaturalism's practical payoff is the hope of divine grace. Grace is needed because evil is powerful (see section 11.2). We are far too weak to have much hope without it. Frodo is wise because he knows this. The whole of Middle-earth—souls as well as bodies—depends on his mission, and he knows he is not strong enough to fulfill it. Yet, because of an implicit trust in grace, he volunteers: "I will take the Ring, though I do not know the way" (LOTR, p. 264). It was a Marian moment. St. Luke showed us the same thing at the Annunciation. Mary's mission was strikingly similar to Frodo's. The salvation of the whole world depended on it. And the words of her acceptance of her mission were also similar to Frodo's: "Let it be to me according to your word" (Lk 1:38).

Neither Tolkien nor St. Luke tells us what invisible force in the soul motivated this visible choice. But there are only two possibilities: pride or humility. When we hear "I will take the ring", we may think we hear pride, but when we hear "though I do not know the way", we know we hear humility. Tolkien kept explicit religion out of *The Lord of the Rings*, but here is a powerful example of implicit religion. No one but an arrogant fool could do what Frodo did without throwing an anchor out into the deep of supernatural grace.

1.3 Are Platonic Ideas real?

When students begin to study the history of philosophy, starting with the ancient Greeks, they are always fascinated with Plato, for two reasons. One is that Plato is not only the first but also the best writer in the history of philosophy. But the other reason is his most distinctive doctrine: Platonic Ideas or Platonic Forms, essences, or archetypes. The theory discombobulates contemporary students because it shows them not only a new doctrine but also a new category, not only a new idea but also a new meaning to the *word* "idea". They feel like the prisoners in the "cave" as they begin to emerge from their comfortable little world of shadows into an alarmingly larger world outside. It is a new metaphysics for them, a new answer to the question "What kinds of things are real; what does 'real' mean?"

Nearly everyone in our culture believes that concrete, individual, material things, like rocks and tigers, are real. (Most Buddhists do not.) Most also believe that there is also another kind of reality, not made of matter: minds, souls, selves, spirits, egos. (Metaphysical materialists like Marxists do not.)

So most people in our culture recognize two kinds of reality, two metaphysical categories: objective matter and subjective spirit, or mind. (If they are very sophisticated they might classify their own bodies as a third category, as subjective matter, and other people's minds as a fourth category, objective spirit.) But Plato offers them a third (or fifth) category, which is objective (unlike minds) but spiritual (unlike material things). And this category is Platonic Ideas. These Ideas are not subjects of thought, not minds; they are objects of thought. But they are not material, spatial, or even temporal objects. For instance, in addition to tigers (material objects) and our subjective minds with their ideas of tigers, there is also Tigerness, the essence of tigers. In addition to rocks there is Rockiness. In addition to good swords and good lawyers and good arguments, there is Goodness itself— not just our ideas of goodness, but the true, objective, eter-

nal, universal, unchangeable essence of goodness itself, which
is dimly reflected or shared ("participated in") in different
ways by good swords and good lawyers and good arguments,
and by our ideas of them.

Platonic Ideas are not things. But they are objectively real.
They are Ideas but not *our* ideas, which change and err. They
are the real truths that measure our ideas as erring or true.
We usually think of ideas as dependent on minds, as acts of
minds, or as opinions in minds, so Platonic Ideas require a
capital *I*; they are neither matter nor mind but a third category of reality. They are real ideals, objective standards.

For instance, when we compare two lines drawn by an
artist and judge that one is straighter than the other, we are
using a standard: the ideal line, the perfectly straight line. No
one has ever seen that. Whatever we can see must reflect
light, which requires a molecular structure, and that requires
three-dimensional matter. But a line is one-dimensional. It is
not a physical thing. But it is not a mere subjective idea in
our minds either. It judges our minds. One mind can be
wrong and another right about what a straight line is, or
about whether line A or line B is straighter. Straightness, or
the Idea of the straight line, is objective to our minds. It is the
perfect standard both for our minds' ideas, and for material
things, both of which are only more or less straight. But
straightness itself is not more or less straight.

All material things are in space and time. All subjective
ideas are in time too, though they are not in space. It takes
time to think as well as to breathe. Platonic Ideas are neither
in space nor in time. They are unchangeable, birthless, and
deathless.

If they exist, where are they? Obviously not anywhere in
space, nor in our minds, but in what? Where is their metaphysical home? Plato never took the next step; he never said

these perfect, unchangeable Ideas must exist in a perfect, unchangeable Mind. But when Christianity entered Greek culture, it supplied the metaphysical house for Plato's Ideas: the Mind of God, the Word of God, the Logos. (And according to the central, essential claim of Christianity, the Word of God is also the Son of God, a divine Person who became incarnate as Jesus Christ, taking a finite, material, mortal human nature.)

These Platonic Ideas vastly expand our vision of what is real by adding the world outside the cave, the Mind of God, the realm of Ideas, and also by transforming this material world into a world of *signs*, not just things. If Plato is right, everything we see is a shadow, copy, image, imitation, or sign of something unseen.

The difference this makes might come clear by a parable:

Once there was a race of rational microorganisms who lived within the index finger on the right hand of a man. The microorganisms carefully explored their world and discovered many of its structures and laws by their science. One day, one of them dared to ask not just a scientific question but a philosophical question; a question about not the parts but the whole. He pursued this question and found that the world as a whole had a shape, a structure: that it was a finger. And it was pointing.

Since all the microorganisms were rational, they were capable of philosophical as well as scientific thinking. Some did not think philosophically at all. Some did, but failed to see that their world was a finger. And some did and saw that their world was a finger. But none of them could see with their science what the finger was pointing to, for all that was visible to their science *was* the finger.

The angels can see what the finger points at, but we microorganisms can't. Our science can't explore the world of

Heavenly archetypes, only the world of material copies. But philosophy can know that this world is a copy of another; philosophy can know that this world is a finger, a sign. In other words, we spiritual microorganisms are less than angels but more than scientists. We are philosophers.

The human experience that helps us best understand Plato's Theory of Ideas is the experience of artistic creativity. Art is very different from science in that it creates worlds; it creates meaning and beauty and forms and structures and natures, while science discovers them. In science, the world is the standard for our ideas about it. If we believe the earth is flat, we are wrong. But in art, it is the reverse: the artist's ideas are the standard for the world he creates. For example, in Tolkien's world, Elves are tall and formidable; in Shakespeare's world, they are tiny and cute. In art, the world conforms to the creative idea; in science, the idea conforms to the world. Truth in science is the reverse of truth in art. If God created the universe, all science is reading God's art.

Heliocentrism, evolution, and relativity are true ideas only if they conform the scientist's mind to the objective physical world; but this world is truly heliocentric, evolutionary, and relative only if it conforms to the divine Idea and design for it. (And everything does that except man. Only in man is there a gap between God's eternal design and temporal fact. The word for that gap is "sin".)

It is because we can look at the things in the universe in this Platonic way that we can rank them. For example, one lion can seem truer, more leonine, than another (say, a weak, scruffy, cowardly lion). We say, "He's a true man", or, "She's a real woman", and that another is false, fake, or inauthentic, like counterfeit money. Counterfeit money is as physically real as real money, yet in the most important way it is *not* real: it does not conform to the Idea of money.

In the case of money the Idea is not Platonic; it is man-made, temporal, and changeable. But in the case of "a real man", a real lion, or a really straight line, the standard is not wholly artificial and relative to different cultures and different individuals. All cultures and all individuals judge a cowardly liar or a cowardly lion to be less authentic, less true, less real than he ought to be. In other words, human minds seem to be in touch with Platonic Ideas when we make value judgments.

Now, in a work of fiction, such as *The Lord of the Rings*, the characters and creatures and landscapes and histories can seem either "fake" (unbelievable, artificial, contrived, inauthentic) or "real" (believable, natural, convincing, authentic), not by conforming to the physical world (except in purely realistic or naturalistic fiction) but by conforming to Platonic Ideas. For instance, Macbeth's three witches are truer, witchier witches than cartoon witches are; and Tolkien's Elves are more real, more elvish than any other writer's elves have ever been. We can't help believing in them. Now, why is that? There are no physical Elves in this world (although most of the citizens of Iceland would disagree with that). So how do we know Tolkien's Elves are more real? We must know the Platonic Idea of Elves, or Elvishness, to be able to use it to compare Tolkien with Shakespeare, for example, and find Shakespeare "elvishly challenged".

Take kingship. Though we do not have kings in America, or want them, our unconscious mind both has them and wants them. We all know what a true king is, a real king, an ideal king, an archetypal king. He is not a mere politician or soldier. Something in us longs to give him our loyalty and fealty and service and obedience. He is lost but longed for and will some day return, like Arthur. In *The Lord of the Rings*, Arthur's name is "Aragorn". When we read *The Lord of the Rings*, he returns to his throne in our minds. He was always there; *The Lord of the Rings* only brings him back into our consciousness from the tomb of the unconscious, where he was sleeping.

Take Hobbits. Why do they strike us as "real"? Where are they? In the Mind of God; and Tolkien knows the Hobbit corner of that Mind better than anyone else. Hobbits are *not* allegories of English farmers, any more than Elves are allegories of Finnish minstrels, or Orcs of Nazi soldiers. They are real because they resemble not physical things or someone's opinions, but Platonic Ideas.

In *The Lord of the Rings* everything seems to be more itself, more Platonic. The earth is more earthy, nature is more natural, the history is more historical, the genealogies more genealogical, the tragedy more tragic, the joy more joyful, the caverns more cavernous, the forests more foresty, and the heroes more heroic. (That is *not* to say they are more one-dimensional, unflawed, and untempted.)

Indeed, the four forests mentioned in *The Lord of the Rings* have more character, more identity than most human characters in most novels. You could not possibly confuse the Old Forest, Lothlorien, Fangorn, and Mirkwood (mentioned in *The Lord of the Rings* but described in *The Hobbit*) with each other. If you found yourself in any one of them, you would instantly know which. When we read *The Lord of the Rings*, why do these forests seem "real" or "true"? Why do we believe them? Not because they are like the forests we have walked through in this world, but because the forests we have walked through in this world were a little like them. Tolkien's forests do not remind us of ours; ours remind us of his.

And this is true of nearly everything in *The Lord of the Rings*. That is one reason why so many inanimate things have names (e.g., swords or horns): because they have individual personalities. The winding Horn of Boromir, the great Horn of Helm, the shrill fire-alarm Horn of Buckland, and the horns the Hobbits use to rouse the Shire at the end are all unforgettable. We have heard their sounds in our hearts, even if we have never heard them in our ears.

Take the sea. To the unimaginative, unpoetic reductionist, the "trousered ape", it is just trillions of tons of H_2O laced with NaCl. But to the poet and the seer, in other words, the normal human being, it is more; it is more like an archetype, and it has inspired longing and desire and exaltation and sadness for millennia. The eye of the poet sees less clearly, but sees farther than the eye of the scientist. As George MacDonald explains,

> Human science is but the backward undoing of the tapestry web of God's science. . . . Is oxygen and hydrogen the divine idea of water? There is no water in oxygen, no water in hydrogen; it comes bubbling fresh from the imagination of the living God, rushing from under the great white throne of the glacier. The very thought of it makes one gasp with an elemental joy.[6]

In *The Allegory of Love*, C. S. Lewis explained the connection between Platonism and Symbolism:

> Symbolism comes to us from Greece. It makes its first effective appearance in European thought with the dialogues of Plato. The Sun is the copy of the Good. Time is the moving image of eternity. All visible things exist just in so far as they succeed in imitating the Forms.[7]

---

[6] Quoted in C. S. Lewis, ed., *George MacDonald: An Anthology* (New York: Macmillan, 1978), no. 185, p. 80.

[7] C. S. Lewis, *The Allegory of Love* (New York: Oxford University Press, 1958), pp. 45–46.

[A Platonic myth] reminds you of something you can't quite place. I think the something is "the whole *quality of life as we actually experience it.*" . . . I've never met Orcs or Ents or Elves—but [I have met] the feel of it, the sense of a huge past, of lowering danger, of heroic feats achieved by the most apparently unheroic people.[8]

The most striking example of this Platonic symbolism in Lewis's own writings, I think, comes at the end of *The Last Battle*, when the whole world of Narnia dies and is swallowed up into its Heavenly Platonic archetype:

"Listen, Peter. When Aslan said you could never go back to Narnia, he meant the Narnia you were thinking of. But that was not the real Narnia. That had a beginning and an end. It was only a shadow or a copy of the real Narnia, which has always been here and always will be here: just as our own world, England and all, is only a shadow or copy of something in Aslan's real world. . . . And of course it is different; as different as a real thing is from a shadow or as waking life is from a dream." His voice stirred everyone like a trumpet as he spoke these words; but when he added under his breath "It's all in Plato, all in Plato: bless me, what *do* they teach them at these schools!" the older ones laughed. It was so exactly like the sort of thing they had heard him say long ago in that other world where his beard was grey instead of golden. . . .

It was the Unicorn who summed up what everyone was feeling. . . . "I have come home at last! This is my real country! I belong here. This is the land I have been looking for all my life, though I never knew it till now. The reason why we loved the old Narnia is that it sometimes looked a little like this." [9]

[8] C. S. Lewis, Letter to Lucy Barfield, 11 September 1958, in *Letters to Children* (New York: Macmillan, 1985), pp. 81–82.

[9] C. S. Lewis, *The Last Battle* (New York, Macmillan, 1956), pp. 160–62.

Notice how the Platonic Ideas in Lewis's concrete literary example moved you more than my abstract philosophical explanations of Plato's Ideas. This is the strategy of the storyteller: to creep past the "watchful dragons" that guard the conscious reason that excludes these things as unbelievable; to open the back door of the heart when the front door of the mind is locked; to appeal to the wiser, deeper, unconscious mind, what Jung called the "collective unconscious". A great mythmaker awakens the longing for these Platonic archetypes, which are buried deep in human knowledge, through using a magic language: the language of myth.

2

Philosophical Theology

"Theology" means thinking or reasoning (*logos*) about God (*theos*). Philosophical theology, or natural theology as distinct from religious theology or supernaturally revealed theology, does not presuppose faith in any religion or religious revelation. It is part of philosophy; its instrument is reason.

Metaphysics is that division of philosophy which deals with being as such, all being, being universally. Philosophical theology is that division of philosophy which deals with what reason can know about the First Being, the Absolute Being, or the Most Perfect Being.

In most Eastern thought there is no distinction between metaphysics and theology because there is no distinction between God and all reality. That is the substance of Eastern enlightenment. God is not thought of as a distinct being who created the universe, but simply as being itself. *Everything* is God, or a manifestation of God, a part of God, or a dream of God. The technical term for this is "pantheism" ("pan" = "everything"). In Western thought, there is a distinction between metaphysics and theology because there is a distinction between being in general and God in particular. In Western paganism there are many gods, who are finite, imperfect beings, part of the sum total of being, while in Jewish, Christian, and Muslim theism, God is the distinct, transcendent Creator of all finite beings.

49

The Lord of the Rings is a book about pagan pre-Christian times written by a Christian. Both the gods of paganism and the God of Christianity are characters in the drama, while pantheism gives you a God who is neither a character nor dramatic. Both paganism and Christianity give you a distinction between God or the gods and other things, and therefore a distinction between metaphysics and theology.

2.1 Does God exist?

The question of whether God really exists is obviously one of the most interesting and important questions in the world for most people, especially for most philosophers. For God's existence or nonexistence makes a difference to everything, since "God" means "the creator and designer and therefore the ultimate explanation for everything". Conversion from atheism to theism, or vice versa, always makes the greatest difference to everything in any person's life.

That includes atheists. Some atheists, including Friedrich Nietzsche and Sartre, are clearer than most theists about God's existence or nonexistence making a total difference to everything. We never appreciate a person so much as when he dies; and Nietzsche applies this to God, who according to Nietzsche is now dead (i.e., the illusion, the faith in God, is dead). The result is that we now feel like a planet detached from its sun, spinning into outer darkness (Nietzsche's image from *The Joyful Wisdom*). For Sartre, the difference God's nonexistence makes is that there can be no eternal truth because there is no divine mind to think it, no objectively real universal moral law because there is no divine will to command it, and no real meaning or purpose to human life because there is no Author to design it (see Sartre's *Existentialism and Human Emotions*).

So the answer to the critic who claims Tolkien never brings God into *The Lord of the Rings* is that He is never out of it. Every one of these fifty philosophical questions would have been answered differently if Tolkien had not believed in God. Can you imagine Sartre or Camus or Beckett writing *The Lord of the Rings*?

God is in *The Silmarillion* explicitly, right from sentence one, as the single Creator, Iluvatar (All-Father). But how is He in *The Lord of the Rings*? Not as a named character, but as the sun is in sunlight. Those with eyes to see can detect His presence everywhere.

Take the Elves, and their songs and their gifts. (I highly recommend you do!) They come from the Blessed Realm, transcendent to Middle-earth, and they "smell" of their origin, trailing clouds of glory. We do not see that origin but we see its effects in Middle-earth, even in natural things ("the heavens declare the glory of God")—for instance, the "light and high beauty" that Sam, stuck in the slag heap of Mordor, suddenly sees in that star whose beams pierce not just his eye but his soul (LOTR, p. 901).

Both atheism and orthodox Jewish, Christian, or Muslim theism are sharp and demanding, often distressing. But many people prefer something in the muddled middle, some compromise that will avoid the demands of both traditional theism and atheism. Increasingly in the West this generic religiosity, or "spirituality", is replacing specific, revealed religion. Bookstores usually have sections on "spirituality" or "New Age" that are much larger than their sections on Christianity.

This newly popular religion is really pantheism. C. S. Lewis explains the difference between pantheism and theism strikingly:

[T]here are things which God is not. In that sense He has a determinate character. Thus He is righteous, not a-moral; creative, not inert. The Hebrew writings here observe an admirable balance. Once God says simply I AM, proclaiming the mystery of self-existence. But times without number He says, "I am the Lord"—I, the ultimate Fact, have *this* determinate character and not *that*. And men are exhorted to "know the Lord," to discover and experience this particular character. . . .

The Pantheist's God does nothing, demands nothing. He is there if you wish for Him, like a book on a shelf. He will not pursue you. There is no danger that at any time heaven and earth should flee away at His glance. If He were the truth, then we could really say that all the Christian images of kingship were a historical accident of which our religion ought to be cleansed. It is with a shock that we discover them to be indispensable. You have had a shock like that before, in connection with smaller matters—when the line pulls at your hand, when something breathes beside you in the darkness. So here; the shock comes at the precise moment when the thrill of *life* is communicated to us along the clue we have been following. It is always shocking to meet life where we thought we were alone. "Look out!" we cry, "it's *alive!*" And therefore this is the very point at which so many draw back—I would have done so myself if I could—and proceed no further with Christianity. An "impersonal God"—well and good. A subjective God of beauty, truth and goodness, inside our own heads—better still. A formless life-force surging through us, a vast power which we can tap—best of all. But God Himself, alive, pulling at the other end of the cord, perhaps approaching at an infinite speed, the hunter, king, husband—that is quite another matter. There comes a moment when the children who have been playing at burglars hush suddenly: was that a *real* footstep in the hall? There comes a moment when people who have been dabbling in religion ("Man's search for

God"!) suddenly draw back. Supposing we really found Him? We never meant it to come to *that*! Worse still, supposing He had found us? (*Miracles*, pp. 87–88, 93–94).

No human author in history has ever successfully portrayed God as a dramatic character. Only the Bible did that; and even there, the Old Testament did it with necessary anthropomorphic inadequacies. But in the New Testament the problem of anthropomorphism is overcome in the most dramatic possible way: God becomes a man, and a man is the one thing impossible to anthropomorphize.

Jesus is certainly a dramatic character. In fact, C. S. Lewis says that everyone who has ever read the Gospels, Plato, and James Boswell will recognize three characters in Heaven: Jesus, Socrates, and Samuel Johnson. But the dramatic character of Jesus is not man's fiction but God's fact. The impossibility of Jesus being a human invention has been a powerful argument for the truth of the Gospels to readers with literary and psychological imagination, like Dostoyevski (this is Dmitri Karamazov's argument) and Kierkegaard (see the last two paragraphs of the first two chapters of *Philosophical Fragments*).[1]

No human author, after the Gospels, has ever successfully portrayed Jesus as a convincing dramatic character. There are only two possible exceptions. One of them is Dostoyevski, in "The Grand Inquisitor", where Christ speaks not one single word. The other is C. S. Lewis, in the Narnia chronicles. Aslan must be Lewis's supreme literary achievement. I know of no other human author who has accomplished what Lewis did: he enabled his readers to experience Christ, to feel toward Aslan as Christ's contemporaries did to Him. How

---

[1] Søren Kierkegaard, *Philosophical Fragments* (Princeton, N.J.: Princeton University Press, 1936, 1962), pp. 24–27, 43–45.

did he do this? By the power of fantasy, which allowed a double distancing: making Christ a lion, not a man, and putting Him in Narnia, not earth.

Tolkien does not portray God in *The Lord of the Rings*, as he does in *The Silmarillion*; and he writes of times long before the Incarnation, so there is no portrayal of Christ. But there are Christ figures, as we shall see in the end (see Chapter 14). In fact, there are Christ figures everywhere in literature and life. This should not surprise us. For Christ was not an emergency afterthought or a freak from outer space, but the central point of the whole human story from the beginning in the Mind of its Author. In fact, Christ *is* the Mind of the Author, the inner Word of God, the Logos.

2.2 Is life subject to divine providence?

Two different ways God can act in earthly history are miracles and providence. There are no miracles in *The Lord of the Rings* (although there are at least two in *The Silmarillion*, at the beginning and the end). But there is a pervasive presence of providence.

God prefers to act by providence rather than miracles, because He loves the natures of all the things He created and wants to perfect them rather than bypass them. He is like a wise, unselfish king Who exalts and empowers His servants rather than distrusting them and micro-managing His kingdom. "Grace perfects nature." It is Sauron who is in love with blatant brute force.

It is easy to identify miracles when we see them, whether worked by God or by evil spirits. But how do we identify divine providence? Where do we find it? Not in a part but in the whole, in the ordering of the whole, in the relationships among the parts. The ultimate reason we find God not only in beings but also in relationships (especially the relationship called love) is that He is not only a Being but also a Society, a Family, a Trinity of Persons.

Whether God exists and whether God acts in the world are two different questions. Deism answers Yes to the first and No to the second. So does pantheism (with a different kind of God). Deism and pantheism are very popular in modern culture for essentially the same reasons Lewis gives in the excerpt quoted above from *Miracles*: "He is there if you wish for Him, like a book on a shelf. He will not pursue you."

However, deism is philosophically closer to theism than pantheism is because deism agrees with theism that there is a transcendent First Cause, a Creator. Both deists and theists use cosmological proofs (proofs from data in the cosmos) to show how reasonable it is to affirm a transcendent being; for example:

1. Nothing can begin without being caused to begin. Nothing simply pops into existence for no reason. That contradicts not only philosophical reason but even scientific reason. If you saw a tiny green rabbit pop into existence on top of this page, would you blandly say, "Oh, well, tiny green rabbits just happen"? Or would you ask, "Why?" Would you look for a cause?

2. And the universe did have a beginning. There were some pretty good philosophical arguments for this conclusion in the Middle Ages, but they did not convince everyone. But today, physical science has discovered convincing evidence that everything—all matter and space and time (which is not absolute and independent of matter but relative to it)—came into existence about fifteen-plus billion years ago. This event, like all events, could not have just happened for no reason at all. It needed a cause adequate to the effect. If there was a Big Bang, there must have been a Big Banger.

3. A nontranscendent being, an immanent being, a part of the universe, could not have caused the whole universe.

4. Therefore there is a transcendent Creator who caused the whole universe.

Theists agree with deists so far. But deists go on to say that this First Cause does not act in the universe. He made the universe and then turned away from it, like a deadbeat dad. But theists believe the Creator also acts on and in His creation, in two ways, and Christians add a third:

First, like an author God designs, knows, arranges, and provides ("providence" = "providing") for everything in His book (the universe). He orders and coordinates all His creatures. No sparrow or hair falls without His providence.

Second, He can and occasionally does intervene with supernatural acts. Some deists admit providence but none admit miracles, as theists do.

Third, Christians also claim that God once inserted Himself into His story as one of His own characters; that Christ was both completely divine and completely human, both transcendent and immanent, both Creator and creature, just as such a self-inserting author would be both the single, unique, transcendent Author outside the book who created it all, and at the same time one of the many immanent characters in the book.

Miracles and the Incarnation are not in *The Lord of the Rings*, but providence certainly is.

If divine providence exists, there should be some evidence for it. Not the kind of evidence we find in mathematics, where a theorem can be proved or disproved with certainty, for all time, to everyone's satisfaction; or even the kind of evidence we find in the physical sciences, where empirical tests can at least definitively refute some hypotheses (e.g., geocentrism, flat earth, six thousand-year-old earth, or parthenogenesis) and the same kind of tests can provide strong empirical evidence, if not certainty, for others (e.g., gravity, relativity, or the Big Bang). But we do find in *The Lord of the Rings* a striking and clearly discernible pattern in the loose threads on the backside of the tapestry.

That image is from Thornton Wilder's *The Bridge of San Luis Rey*. God's design for history is like a tapestry, and only He sees it clearly, from the front, finished side. But there are enough clues on the backside, enough *effects* of divine providence, to elicit and justify a rational faith, though not enough for proof. Reason leaves this question open so that we can believe if we want to, so that faith is a free option, but not a compulsion. God seduces our wills but does not force them. As Blaise Pascal says, there is just enough light for seekers and not so much that even nonseekers are compelled against their will.

When Christianity displaced paganism in the ancient West, it *added* many beliefs and categories, such as monotheism, creation, the Trinity, the Incarnation, salvation, divine love, and universal human dignity (for all persons are created in the image of God and destined for eternal union with Him); but it also *subtracted* two pagan concepts: *fate* and *chance*. In paganism, fate was believed to be a power above even the gods, and chance was believed to control many events in life that were not known or designed by either men or gods. But if an all-knowing God created and designed the entire universe, then blind fate and blind chance are exiled as much as pagan gods like Zeus and Pan are. ("Great Pan is dead", announced the pagan prophet, because he had been displaced by Christ—as Nietzsche was to claim, centuries later, that the Christian "God is dead.") The single divine light is totalizing, and all darkness flees before it. At the beginning of the Christian era fate and chance fled before providence.

The commonest examples of divine providence in our experience are remarkable "coincidences". For instance, the squirrel that just "happened" to drop a nut onto a fallen leaf in the park just at the right place and time, a century ago, made the young man who was going to be your grandfather turn his head to the sound and thus just "happen" to notice for the first time the girl who was going to be your grandmother, who just "happened" to be walking by, and one thing led to another so that eventually you were born. Most of us exist only because such things have "happened"—or been very cleverly and anonymously arranged. To quote *The Bridge of San Luis Rey*, "Some say that to the gods we are like flies idly swatted by boys on a summer day. Others say that not a hair falls to the ground from our head without the will of the Heavenly Father." [2]

There is no strict logical proof of divine providence. You "just see it", or else not, as you see the pattern in the tapestry or hear it in a piece of music. You can see the hand of providence more clearly if you become more familiar with it, like the face of a stranger who becomes a friend. It is a *gestalt*, a pattern connecting many particular things and events, not a marked-out particular thing or event. It cannot be assembled or constructed by analysis, step by step. It becomes much clearer to us *after* the event than before; for our hindsight is keener than our foresight. That is why Prometheus ("foresight") is more godlike than Epimetheus ("after-sight").

The Lord of the Rings is chock-full of divine providences. In fact, if there is any one particular religious doctrine that is as large as a continent in *The Lord of the Rings*, this is it. It is "like the sky, spread over everything". [3] One could write an entire

[2] Thornton Wilder, *The Bridge of San Luis Rey* (New York: Albert and Charles Boni, 1928), pp. 19, 23.

[3] C. S. Lewis, *A Grief Observed* (New York: Seabury Press, 1961), p. 13.

book on this theme alone. I will make this section very short precisely because it could be so long.

The most remarkable examples surround evils, events that seem very bad when they occur, yet which turn out to have been for the best, just as Romans 8:28 asserts. For instance, Frodo rightly sees his finding of the Ring as the worst thing that has ever happened to him: "I was not made for perilous quests. I wish I had never seen the Ring. Why did it come to me?" (LOTR, p. 60). Yet Gandalf sees the providential good even in this evil, in fact, especially in this:

> "It was not Gollum, Frodo, but the Ring itself that decided things. The Ring left *him*. . . . There was more than one power at work, Frodo. The Ring was trying to get back to its master . . . [but behind] that there was something else at work, beyond any design of the Ring-maker. I can put it no plainer than by saying that Bilbo was *meant* to find the Ring, and *not* by its maker. In which case you also were *meant* to have it. And that may be an encouraging thought" (LOTR, pp. 54–55).

Note, in this passage (1) how the interplay between the intentions of Gollum, Bilbo, Frodo, Sauron, and the Ring itself are all instruments of the intentions of "something else at work"; (2) how the presence of this "something else" (divine providence) is sensed even when not named; (3) how much more effective it is for Tolkien not to name it, not to tell but to show, to give us just the back side of the tapestry, not the cause but the effects, not the explanation but just the data; and (4) how "encouraging" this is, if this "something else" is good rather than evil.

Tolkien himself interprets the climax of the plot providentially: "Frodo had done what he could and spent himself completely (as an instrument of divine Providence) and had produced a situation in which the object of his quest could be achieved. His humility (with which he began) and his sufferings were justly rewarded by the highest honour; and his exercise of patience and mercy toward Gollum gained him Mercy: his failure (at the Cracks of Doom) was redressed" (*Letters*, no. 246, p. 326).

In *The Lord of the Rings* there are literally hundreds of providential "coincidences" (see the Concordance, II.A.) Yet they are not preachy, contrived, unbelievable, forced, or allegorical. They are not a jimmying of the plot, as in the pious potboilers of Frank Perretti or Tim LaHaye. And this narrative credibility, this naturalness, is itself a strong argument for the truth of the doctrine. It is "true to life". This is one of the ways in which literature can persuade us more powerfully than logic.

For instance, I was never persuaded by any argument of the truth of the apparently ridiculous idea that each of us is responsible for all the evil done in the world; but Dostoyevski not only *told* it but *sold* it because he *showed* it to be true, in *The Brothers Karamazov*. Reading that book was like meeting an animal I had thought to be mythical. It was leaping into my life, out of its picture book: "Good grief! Giant squids aren't myths. There's one of them."

Of course, Tolkien did not set out to write "a book about providence". The belief structured his unconscious as well as conscious mind, and thus naturally structured the plot that he allowed to unfold in its own way—a way that surprised him as well as his readers.

C. S. Lewis articulated the orthodox Christian doctrine of divine providence thus:

> Unless we are to abandon the conception of Providence altogether . . . all events are equally providential. If God directs the course of events at all then he directs the

movement of every atom at every moment; "not one sparrow falls to the ground" without that direction. . . . This may sound excessive, but in reality we are attributing to the Omniscient only an infinitely superior degree of the same kind of skill which a mere human novelist exercises daily in constructing his plot. . . . In the play *Hamlet*, . . . [e]very event in the play happens as a result of other events in the play, but also every event happens because the poet wants it to happen. . . . "Providence" and Natural causation are not alternatives; both determine every event (*Miracles*, pp. 174–75, 179).

2.3 Are we both fated and free?

Closely connected to the idea of providence is the puzzle of free will and its relation to fate, or destiny, or predestination. ("Destiny" seems the most generic term, "fate" having more specifically pagan and "predestination" more specifically Christian connotations.) It is one of the most obvious and most often-asked questions in philosophy.

The Lord of the Rings is dense with destiny. Though the events are surprises to the reader, as to the protagonists, they also form a pattern, and we eventually see that they all "had" to happen that way. None of the endings, happy or sad, are unconvincing, unnatural, or unbelievable (though they are unpredictable). Sauron *had* to fall. At least some of the Hobbits *had* to rise to the heroic occasion. Sacrifices *had* to be made. Battles *had* to be fought. And it was predictable that the unpredictable would happen.

On the other hand, the protagonists make hundreds of free choices, some large, some small; and even the small ones make large differences. For instance, just one page after Frodo leaves Bag End, singing his Road song, he hears a horse on the road. Apparently Gandalf is coming. But Frodo suddenly desires to hide. At this point Frodo does not know the danger of the Black Riders; but had he not hid, the Quest would have ended then and there. The Rider would have captured Frodo and the Ring, delivered both to Sauron, and Middle-earth would have become Hell on earth.

Nearly everyone believes in free will, at least until he meets arguments against it, either from social scientists who claim that all our choices can be explained by heredity plus environment, or from philosophers who begin with the false assumption that a human choice must be either (1) caused, and thus determined, and thus necessitated, and thus unfree, or else (2) free and thus uncaused—but something uncaused is unintelligible. The answer to both is that "free causality" is not a self-contradiction but a uniquely human kind of causality.

We believe in free will because we directly experience it. We all know the difference between being free and being forced. Sometimes a thing is in our power or control, and sometimes not. There is also a middle case, when we are at the mercy of a force but the force is internal, like an addiction. (This is the case with the Ring.) It is *our* addiction, not another's, and if we had made different free choices in the past, we might not have it; yet it removes our freedom. Sometimes we freely sell ourselves into slavery.

But we also naturally believe in something like destiny. "It was meant to be", we say. It is not so clear why we naturally believe this, but we do. Probably because we unconsciously realize that the alternative is meaningless chaos, not a story.

So we wonder how both can be true, since the two ideas seem to contradict each other. Does destiny, or God, or fate pull my strings, or do I pull my own strings with my free will?

There are good philosophical arguments for believing both, and for believing that the two ideas do not contradict each other. I shall give two of them in a moment. But the strongest, most convincing evidence comes not from philosophers but from storytellers. Both of these ingredients, free will and destiny, are always present in every successful story, every interesting story, every (and this is the point) story we find *realistic*, "true to life". A story without predestination means a story without an author, and that is a story without any authority. But a story without free will, a story about machines or falling raindrops, is not a story either. Every story has to have in it free persons making free choices that they could have made differently—otherwise there is no drama.

Every story has to have a plot, and thus a plotter, and thus destiny. Authors can be *bad* plotters, plodding plotters, and their stories can turn out not just sadly but badly. Authors can commit destiny fallacies just as philosophers can commit logical fallacies. For instance, it is Ahab's destiny to be swallowed by Moby Dick, and there would be a "destiny fallacy" if Ahab had listened to some pop psychologist, been cured of his obsession, seen the error of his ways, and become "*Nice* Captain Ahab"—just as there would be a "destiny fallacy" if Scrooge had exorcised the Ghost of Christmas Future, put Bob Cratchit in the poorhouse, and become the Godfather of the London Mafia.

We may not know *how* destiny and freedom can both be true, but we know that they must both be present in true-to-life stories because they are both present in life.

Sometimes philosophers can help. Here are two philosophical arguments to explain how both of these ideas can be true without contradiction:

The first is the principle that divine grace, in dealing with anything in nature, does not suppress or bypass its nature but perfects it and works through it. (A human author does the same thing with his characters.) Therefore, divine predestination preserves human free will, because God invented it. As Aquinas says, man is free *because* God is all-powerful. For God not only gets everything done that He designs, but also gets everything done in the right way: subhuman things happen unfreely, and human things happen freely. Just as in a novel, the setting is not free and the characters are.

The second philosophical argument (from Boethius's *Consolation of Philosophy*) is that since God is not in time, destiny does not mean *pre*destination, like pushing dominoes. As usual, C. S. Lewis summarizes this point as clearly as anyone has done:

> God is not in Time. . . . He has all eternity in which to listen to the split second of prayer put up by a pilot as his plane crashes in flames. . . .
>
> God is not hurried along in the Time-stream of this universe any more than an author is hurried along in the imaginary time of his own novel. He has infinite attention to spare for each one of us. . . . You are as much alone with Him as if you were the only being He had ever created. When Christ died, He died for you individually just as much as if you had been the only man in the world. . . .
>
> [I]f God *foresaw* our acts, it would be very hard to understand how we could be free not to do them. But suppose God is outside and above the Time-line. In that case, what we call "tomorrow" is visible to Him in just the same way as what we call "today." All the days are "Now" for Him. He does not remember you doing things yesterday; He simply sees you doing them, because, though you have lost yesterday, He has not. He does not "foresee" you doing things tomorrow; He simply sees you doing

them; because, though tomorrow is not yet there for you, it is for Him. You never suppose that your actions at this moment were any less free because God knows what you are doing. Well, He knows your tomorrow's actions in just the same way—because He is already in tomorrow and can simply watch you.[4]

2.4 Can we relate to God by "religion"?

Because *The Lord of the Rings* takes place in pre-Christian times, it could not be a Christian book without anachronism. But it is religious:

> It is a monotheistic world of "natural theology." The odd fact that there are no churches, temples, or religious rites and ceremonies, is simply part of the historical climate depicted. . . . I am in any case a Christian, but the "Third Age" was not a Christian world (*Letters*, no. 165, p. 220).

Flannery O'Connor defined the Christian novel not as a novel about Christianity, Christians, or a Christian world, but "one in which the truth as Christians know it has been used as a light to see the world by".[5] Light "looked along" instead of "looked at": this is exactly Lewis's image in "Meditation in a Toolshed" (see section 6.2). A universal light from an invisible source: this is almost exactly the image Sam uses for Lothlorien (see LOTR, p. 351; see also page 69, below, where it is also the image an agnostic reader of *The Lord of the Rings* used in a letter to Tolkien for the theism of the whole book [*Letters*, no. 328, p. 413]).

[4] C. S. Lewis, *Mere Christianity*, rev. ed. (New York: Macmillan, 1952), pp. 146–49.
[5] Flannery O'Connor, *Mystery and Manners* (New York: Farrar, Straus and Giroux, 1962), p. 173.

The absence of temples, rites, and ceremonies does not make *The Lord of the Rings* nonreligious, but there is one religious act whose absence *does* seem to make *The Lord of the Rings* nonreligious. That act is prayer. Prayer is near the heart of religion, because "religion" means "relationship", or "binding relationship", between God and man (or Elf or Hobbit). Prayer touches the life of everyone except atheists. Therefore, with incredible irony, Hollywood "corrected" Tolkien here by *adding* this religious element: Arwen's prayer for the dying Frodo after the Morgul knife pierced him at Weathertop. Is Hollywood more religious than Tolkien? No, just more overt. Peter Jackson put prayer back into the surface of the story because the surface is where movie audiences live. But he put it into the surface because he sensed that it was already there at the heart of the story.

We can distinguish four ways a story can be religious, corresponding to Aristotle's Four Causes. A story can be religious (1) in its material cause, or subject matter; (2) in its final cause, or purpose; (3) in its formal cause, or structure; or (4) in its efficient cause, or origin.

1. *The Lord of the Rings* is not religious in its subject matter: it is not *about* religion. But the reason for this, according to Tolkien's explicit strategy, is to make the story *more* religious:

> *The Lord of the Rings* is of course a fundamentally religious and Catholic work; unconsciously so at first but consciously in the revision. I . . . therefore have cut out practically all references to anything like "religion," to cults and practices in the imaginary world, for the religious element is absorbed into the story and the symbolism (*Letters*, no. 156, p. 201).

> I have deliberately written a tale which is built on or out of certain "religious" ideas, but is *not* an allegory of them (*Letters*, no. 211, p. 283).

I have purposely kept all allusions to the highest matters down to mere hints, perceptible only by the most attentive. . . . So God and the angelic gods, . . . only peep through in such places as Gandalf's conversation with Frodo: "behind that there was something else at work, beyond any design of the Ring-maker's"; or in Faramir's Numenorean grace at dinner (*Letters*, no. 156, p. 201).

The Lord of the Rings is a myth, and myth is naturally religious. Tolkien writes, "Something really 'higher' is occasionally glimpsed in mythology: Divinity, the right to power (as distinct from its possession), the due worship; in fact 'religion'" ("On Fairy-Stories", p. 25).

To readers or critics who insist that *The Lord of the Rings* is not a religious book, and therefore the question of God's existence is irrelevant to it, Tolkien himself replies that the main character of *The Lord of the Rings* is God, and the main issue is God's honor:

In *The Lord of the Rings* the conflict is not basically about "freedom," though that is naturally involved. It is about God, and His sole right to divine honour. . . . Sauron desired to be a God-King. . . . If he had been victorious he would have demanded divine honour from all rational creatures and absolute temporal power over the whole world (*Letters*, no. 183, pp. 243–44).

So the most fundamental conflict in *The Lord of the Rings* is religious? Of course! Why else is Sauron's desire to play God by using the Ring evil unless it is contrary to reality, that is, unless God is real and only God is God? It is a very simple and obvious point, and an absolutely central one to the story and to its central symbol, the Ring. Yet it will sound shocking to those who cannot admit loving anything "religious" but cannot help loving *The Lord of the Rings*.

2. *The Lord of the Rings* is not religious in its conscious, originating motive and purpose. Tolkien did not begin by saying, "Let's see now; I'd like to convert people or make them saints. How shall I do it? Let's try a story."

Yet he did declare, to one critic, "I would claim . . . to have as one object the elucidation of truth and the encouragement of good morals in the real world by the ancient device of exemplifying them in unfamiliar embodiments, that may tend to 'bring them home'" (*Letters*, no. 153, p. 194). This end does not necessarily require either allegory or conscious "moralism" as its means.

3. The main way *The Lord of the Rings* is religious is in its form, its structure: (a) of its worldview and thus of its world, its setting, the world of Middle-earth; (b) of the plot, full of providential design and cosmic justice; and (c) of the characters as manifesting themes like providence, grace, heroism, hierarchy, glory, resurrection, piety, duty, authority, obedience, tradition, humility, and "eucatastrophe" (see section 5.1). All these themes (which we will explore later in this book) have a religious dimension.

If the antireligious person loves this story, he must unconsciously love the Christian story, not because *The Lord of the Rings* is an allegory of Christianity but because its author's mind and philosophy are one with that of the Author of the Christian story.

Take a specific instance. Nonreligious people usually believe in compassion and mercy, but not that mercy will be rewarded, if there is no God. But Christianity knows it will, even in this world, because the plot of human history is written by a God Who loves mercy. Thus the apparently foolish mercy that spares Gollum time after time is rewarded at the Crack of Doom. The reader sees that, at least unconsciously, and if his heart is open to loving that, he is on the way to believing and loving the God Who is behind that "mercy system" whose literal Crack of Doom in our world was Calvary.

4. *The Lord of the Rings* may also be religious in its efficient cause, i.e., something like divine inspiration. Tolkien wrote of a visitor who startled him by saying:

> "Of course you don't suppose, do you, that you wrote all that book yourself?" Pure Gandalf! I was too well acquainted with G. . . . to ask what he meant. I think I said: "No, I don't suppose so any longer." I have never since been able to suppose so. An alarming conclusion for an old philologist to draw concerning his private amusement. But not one that should puff any one up who considers the imperfections of "chosen instruments." . . .
> You speak of "a sanity and sanctity" in *The L.R.* "which is a power in itself." I was deeply moved. Nothing of the kind had been said to me before. But by a strange chance, just as I was beginning this letter, I had one from a man, who classified himself as "an unbeliever, or at best a man of belatedly and dimly dawning religious feeling. . . . But you," he said, "create a world in which some sort of faith seems to be everywhere without a visible source, like light from an invisible lamp." I can only answer: "Of his own sanity no man can securely judge. If sanctity inhabits his work or as a pervading light illumines it then it does not come from him but through him. And neither of you would perceive it in these terms unless it was with you also" (*Letters*, no. 328, p. 413).

"Light from an invisible lamp"—that is almost exactly Sam's description of the Elvish forest of Lorien:

> "If there's any magic about, it's right down deep, where I can't lay my hands on it, in a manner of speaking."

"You can see and feel it everywhere," said Frodo.

"Well," said Sam, "you can't see nobody working it" (LOTR, p. 351).

Exactly the way God runs the universe.

3

Angelology

3.1 Are angels real?

Of all the divisions of philosophy in our outline, this one is certain to seem the most surprising, suspicious, or even bizarre. Why?

Not because angels are not in themselves important enough to deserve a philosophical science (angelology). For if they really exist, they are in many ways to us what we are to animals: the next step up on the cosmic hierarchy, immensely more intelligent, powerful, and beautiful than we are, the most Godlike creatures that exist. And they make a far greater difference to our lives than we suspect.

Angels are forgotten by modern philosophy not because they are unfashionable: they are not unfashionable. They have returned to popular culture with an exclamation point. But the wave of interest in them has not yet hit the beach of philosophers.

Nearly every pre-modern culture has believed that something like angels (superhuman spirits) exist and are prior to man both in rank and in time. We find them at the beginning of the real world and also at the beginning of Tolkien's fictional world in *The Silmarillion.* We also find them inspiring the beginning of Tolkien's writing of this fictional world, during World War I, when he was haunted by a single line in an eighth-century Anglo-Saxon poem by Cynewulf entitled

"Crist". The line was: "Hail Earendil, brightest of Angels, Over Middle-earth sent unto men." Tolkien wrote, "I felt a curious thrill as if something had stirred in me, half wakened from sleep. There was something very remote and strange and beautiful behind those words, if I could grasp it, far beyond the ancient English." [1]

The word "angel" means "messenger". It tells the angels' job description, not their essence. As to their essence, the mainline Christian tradition says that angels are pure spirits, with no kind of bodies, while a secondary tradition says they have "spiritual bodies". Whichever of these is Tolkien's view, it is clear that the angels in *The Lord of the Rings* (who are the Wizards, the Istari) did not get their bodies from nature, from sex, or from parents. They have no parents and no children.

In *The Silmarillion* the angels are named "the Ainur". Those who enter the created world are called "the Valar". The lesser ranks of the Valar are the Maiar. Some of the Maiar become Istari, or Wizards, like Gandalf. They are guardian angels, and they carry out divine providence by guiding and guarding man, just as in the Jewish, Christian, and Muslim Scriptures and traditions. In all three traditions, and in *The Silmarillion*, God creates angels before He creates the material universe. But in *The Silmarillion* He then uses the angels as instruments in creating the material world. This idea, while not part of the mainline Christian tradition, is not heretical. It is a *theologoumenon* (a possible theological opinion) that is found in some of the Church Fathers. And it helps to solve a difficult aspect of the "problem of evil", the problem of reconciling real evil with an all-good and all-powerful God. Moral evil can be traced to human sin, but where did physi-

[1] Stratford Caldecott, "The Horns of Hope: J. R. R. Tolkien and the Heroism of Hobbits", *The Chesterton Review*, vol. 28, nos. 1 and 2 (Feb./May 2002), South Orange, N.J.: Seton Hall University, 2002.

cal evils come from? If God entrusted the shaping of the material world to angels, then since the fall of the angels came before the fall of man, they may have had a hand in the world's "thorns and thistles". Though most modern theologians do not even mention this solution, C. S. Lewis refers to it respectfully in *The Problem of Pain*.

In *The Silmarillion*, the Ainur can put on human bodies as we put on clothes. This is also a *theologoumenon*. Certain biblical passages seem to imply it: the Nephilim in Genesis 6, the three angels eating Abraham's food in Genesis 19, and Tobias being guided by the angel in disguise (Tobit 5–12).

In *The Silmarillion*,[2] those Ainur who enter the world become the Valar, the Powers of the World, and remain with it until the world's end. These, Tolkien says, "Men have often called gods" (p. 25), thus offering a more-than-psychological explanation for ancient polytheism.

Angels can bilocate. They can live both in Heaven and on earth at the same time. The most important angel in *The Lord of the Rings*, next to Gandalf, is Elbereth, who also bilocates, for she saves Frodo at the Ford of Bruinen and again in Shelob's lair, but she is also Varda, Lady of the Stars.

The angels are the main protagonists of the first two parts of *The Silmarillion* ("Ainulindale" and "Valequenta"), the Elves are the main protagonists of most of the rest of *The Silmarillion*, and Hobbits are the main protagonists of *The Lord of the Rings*. But angels are certainly not absent from *The Lord of the Rings*. The Wizards, including Gandalf and Saruman, are angels, of the lower order of Maiar; Sauron and also the Balrogs are fallen, evil Maiar (*Silmarillion*, p. 31); and Tom Bombadil and Goldberry are quite possibly the Valar Aulë and Yavanna (ibid., pp. 27–28, 39).

---

[2] J. R. R. Tolkien, *The Silmarillion*, ed. Christopher Tolkien (Boston: Houghton Mifflin, 1977).

Tolkien and C. S. Lewis read their manuscripts aloud to each other at meetings of the Inklings (an informal literary group) while Tolkien was working on *The Lord of the Rings* and Lewis on his space trilogy. So there are bound to be many influences, some conscious, some not. Decide for yourself, by instinct or your innate "angel detector", how similar Lewis's angels are to Tolkien's. For myself, I find no two writers' angels more compelling and believable.

Here is a philosophical argument for them (or against the prejudice against them) from Lewis's *Miracles*:

> The mere idea of a . . . reality which is "supernatural" in relation to the world of our five present senses but "natural" from its own point of view, is profoundly shocking to a certain philosophical preconception. . . . [W]e are prepared to believe either in a reality with one floor or a reality with two floors, but not in a reality like a skyscraper with several floors. . . . That is why many believe in God who cannot believe in angels and an angelic world. . . . I cannot now understand, but I well remember, the passionate conviction with which I myself once defended this prejudice. . . . Yet it is very difficult to see any rational grounds for the dogma that reality must have no more than two levels. There cannot, from the nature of the case, be evidence that God never created and will never create, more than one system (*Miracles*, pp. 153–55).

3.2 Do we have guardian angels?

The leader of the Fellowship and of the opposition against Sauron is a guardian angel. Tolkien says of Gandalf,

> He was an *incarnate* "angel" . . . sent to Middle-earth, as the great crisis of Sauron loomed on the horizon. By "incarnate" I mean they were embodied in physical bod-

ies capable of pain, and weariness, and of afflicting the
spirit with physical fear, and of being "killed". . . . Why
they should take such a form is . . . precisely to limit and
hinder their exhibition of "power" on the physical plane,
and so that they should do what they were primarily sent
for: train, advise, instruct, arouse the hearts and minds of
those threatened by Sauron to a resistance with their own
strengths, and not just to do the job for them (*Letters*, no.
156, p. 202).

Before September 11, 2001, most of us saw America as the
Hobbits saw the Shire,

> as a district of well-ordered business; and there in that
> pleasant corner of the world they plied their well-ordered
> business of living; and they heeded less and less the world
> outside where dark things moved, until they came to
> think that peace and plenty were the rule in Middle-earth
> and the right of all sensible folk. They forgot or ignored
> what little they had ever known of the Guardians, and of
> the labours of those that made possible the long peace of
> the Shire. They were, in fact, sheltered, but they had
> ceased to remember it (LOTR, p. 5).

Tolkien believed that we too have guardians, and they are
not the CIA or the FBI. We are guarded not by guardian
agents but by guardian angels. And it is good to know a little
about them—but not too much. For, as Pippin says, " 'We
can't live long on the heights.' 'No,' said Merry. 'I can't. Not
yet, at any rate. But at least, Pippin, we can now see them,
and honour them . . . and not a gaffer could tend his garden
in what he calls peace but for them, whether he knows about
them or not. I am glad I know about them a little' " (LOTR,
p. 852). And so are we.

The highest of the "guardian angels" in *The Lord of the
Rings* is Elbereth. At the most critical juncture in the Quest,

Sam is inspired to invoke her by name, "speaking in tongues" (language is always the clearest indicator of importance in Tolkien):

> A Elbereth Gilthoniel
> o menel palan-diriel,
> le nallon sí di-nguruthos!
> A tiro nin, Fanuilos! (LOTR, p. 712)

This translates as: "O Elbereth Starkindler from heaven gazing-afar, to thee I cry now in the shadow of death. O look towards me, Everwhite."

Indeed, Tolkien writes, "I am a Christian (which can be deduced from my stories), and in fact a Roman Catholic. The latter 'fact' perhaps cannot be deduced; though one critic (by letter) asserted that the invocations of Elbereth, and the character of Galadriel . . . were clearly related to Catholic devotion to Mary" (*Letters*, no. 213, p. 288). Tolkien introduces Elbereth in *The Silmarillion* as "Varda, Lady of the Stars, who knows all the regions of Ea. Too great is her beauty to be declared in the words of Men, or of Elves; for the light of Iluvatar lives still in her face. In light is her power and her joy" (*Silmarillion*, p. 27). He also says of Galadriel: "I think it is true that I owe much of this character to Christian and Catholic teaching and imagination about Mary" (*Letters*, no. 220, p. 407). And he writes to Fr. Robert Murray, S.J., "I think I know exactly what you mean by the order of Grace; and of course by your references to Our Lady, upon which all my own small perception of beauty both in majesty and simplicity is founded" (*Letters*, no. 142, p. 172).

C. S. Lewis was not a Roman Catholic; in fact, he treated the Roman Catholic Church as an Irishman afraid of marriage treats a woman. He did not have the "Marian" dimension that Tolkien had. (Yet a doctoral dissertation entitled "The Marian Dimension in the Writings of C. S. Lewis" was written at Rome's Gregorian University.) But he did have the "angelic" dimension Tolkien had, especially regarding guardian angels. In *The Screwtape Letters*, Lewis looks through the eyes of Screwtape, a senior demon writing to his apprentice demon, Wormwood, whose human patient has just died in the state of grace, and he imagines what it will be like for us to see our guardian angels when we die, and to know their role in our lives:

"You have let a soul slip through your fingers. . . . How well I know what happened at the instant when they snatched him from you! There was a sudden clearing of the eyes (was there not?) as he saw you for the first time, and recognized the part you had had in him and knew that you had it no longer. . . .

"As he saw you, he also saw Them. I know how it was. You reeled back dizzy and blinded. . . . The degradation of it!—that this thing of earth and slime could stand upright and converse with spirits before whom you, a spirit, could only cower. . . . When he saw them he knew that he had always known them and realized what part each one of them had played at many an hour in his life when he had supposed himself alone, so that now he could say to them, one by one, not 'Who *are* you?' but 'So it was *you* all the time'. . . . The dim consciousness of friends about him which had haunted his solitudes from infancy was now at last explained; that central music in every pure experience which has always just evaded memory was now at last recovered." [3]

[3] C. S. Lewis, *The Screwtape Letters* (New York: Macmillan, 1957), pp. 156–59.

3.3 Could there be creatures between men
     and angels, such as Elves?

One reason Tolkien did not bring the Valar (angels) more
directly into *The Lord of the Rings* is that they would have
"lowered" the Elves, made them less distinguishable from
Men, less awesome, less like angels. For Elves are semiangelic
beings in *The Lord of the Rings*, both in themselves and to us.
In themselves because they are semi-immortal; to us because
when we look at them we look *in the direction of* the angels,
just as when a crab looks up from the bottom of a pool at the
fish swimming near the water's surface it looks in the direction of the birds, air, and light.

Elves are not, like the Ainur, pure spirits that can assume
bodies as we assume clothing. Nor are they mortals like us.
Their bodies are immortal as long as the matter of the world
lasts, and if their bodies are killed in Middle-earth, their
spirits return to the Halls of Mandos and are given new
bodies by reincarnation.

Tolkien writes, "The Elves represent . . . the artistic, aesthetic, and purely scientific aspects of the Humane [*sic*] Nature raised to a higher level than is actually seen in Men"
(*Letters*, no. 181, p. 236). The movie has them fight alongside
Men (and Dwarf) at Helm's Deep—a legitimate extension of
the friendship between Legolas and Gimli—to show the
alliance of all the good species and the involvement of all in
the spiritual warfare that is the main theme of history.

One reason both Elves and Dwarves are so common in
pre-modern literature is that they represent, roughly, the
spiritual and the physical, soul and body, angel-like and
animal-like halves of human nature. In *The Lord of the Rings*,
however, the contrast is more between Elves and Hobbits,

who are neither artists nor scientists nor seers, but humble, earthy, "bourgeois", creature-comfort-loving homebodies. An author succeeds if we recognize parts of ourselves in each character; but Tolkien aims higher· we recognize parts of ourselves in each *species*.

Elves and fairies are not quite synonymous, but they are overlapping; and when Tolkien writes the most insightful essay ever written about fairy tales, he is writing about Elves. Indeed, he makes the connection explicitly:

> "Faërian Drama"—those plays which according to abundant records the elves have often presented to men—can produce Fantasy with a realism and immediacy beyond the compass of any human mechanism. As a result their usual effect (upon a man) is to go beyond Secondary Belief [literary belief]. If you are present at a Faërian drama you yourself are, or think that you are, bodily inside its Secondary World [as the four Hobbits felt at Tom Bombadil's house in *The Fellowship of the Ring*, chap. 7]. . . . To the elvish craft, Enchantment, Fantasy aspires, and when it is successful of all forms of human art most nearly approaches ("On Fairy-Stories", pp. 51–53).

Here is the clue that solves the great Tolkien puzzle. The puzzle is why, of all humans who ever took pen to paper, Tolkien has produced by far the most convincing, desirable, beautiful, believable, and awesome Elves. And the answer is that he must have been an Elf. Or at least he had Elf blood somewhere in his ancestry. For if any work of literature in the history of the world is a "Faërian drama", it is *The Lord of the Rings*.

The existence of Elves, or something like Elves, is widespread in pre-modern cultures. (And over half of the world's most literate nation, Iceland, still believes in them; that's why their wilderness roads take sudden turns, to avoid disturbing them.) When the word is used today, most people snicker. But most pre-modern accounts are far more angelic, more transcendent, more wonderful, more *formidable*, than the silly Tinkerbells of modern literature.

Tolkien writes that "they represent really Men with greatly enhanced aesthetic and creative faculties, greater beauty and longer life, and nobility—the Elder Children, doomed to fade before the Followers" (*Letters,* no. 144, p. 176). Nobility, but not perfection. In *The Silmarillion,* the Elves' history, like ours, is mainly war, tragedy, and darkness. They envy us our mortality, as we envy them their immortality. (Envy is one of the stupidest of sins, the only one that never caused a single moment of even false joy.) Though Tolkien is both temperamentally and ideologically conservative, the Elves are bad conservatives: they want to embalm the present. Seeing the downward slant of the present, they try to preserve the past. They are not *evil* like Sauron, who always wants to sing "I Did It My Way", but they are *foolish* because they sing "I Believe in Yesterday". We too are foolishly Elvish when we want to hold onto our youth, or the initial experience of falling in love, or when we seek the enoughness of eternity that we all innately long for in places where it can never be, somewhere in time.

The same philosophical arguments for the existence of angels that we saw C. S. Lewis use (see section 3.1) could also be used as probable arguments for the possible existence of Elves or other species between the human and the angelic.

Though C. S. Lewis never wrote about Elves as such, either in his fiction or in his nonfiction, he did nicely summarize what humanity has thought of them in *The Discarded Image,* in the chapter on the *Longaevi,* or longlivers (pp. 122–38):

Their unimportance is their importance. They are marginal, fugitive creatures. . . . Herein lies their imaginative value. They soften the classic severity of the huge [cosmic] design. They intrude a welcome hint of wildness and uncertainty into a universe that is in danger of being a little too self-explanatory, too luminous. . . .

There was sufficient belief to produce rival theories of their nature; . . .

(1) That they are a third rational species distinct from angels and men. . . .

(2) That they are angels, but a special class of angels who have been, in our jargon, "demoted". . . .

(3) That they are the dead, or some special class of the dead. . . .

(4) That they are fallen angels; in other words, devils. . . .

No agreement was achieved. As long as the Fairies remained at all they remained evasive.[4]

---

[4] C. S. Lewis, *The Discarded Image* (Cambridge, Eng.: Cambridge University Press, 1967), pp. 122, 134, 136–38.

4

Cosmology

Cosmology is a division of philosophy seldom seen anymore because most philosophers think its questions have all been answered by the natural sciences, ever since the discovery of the modern scientific method.

But there are certainly some questions about the cosmos that the physical sciences do not have the method for answering, while philosophy does: for instance, the justification of principles science takes for granted, such as the uniformity of nature, causality, and the correlation between objective intelligibility in nature and subjective intelligence in man's mind, as well as nonquantifiable questions like the beauty and value of nature, and why we find a mysterious nonutilitarian joy in things like forests, stars, and storms.

4.1 Is nature really beautiful?

Unlike much science fiction, fantasy uses realistic settings. Middle-earth is our earth. It is not a never-never land, or even another planet. It is not a different place, only a different time. The setting of Tolkien's fantasies is literally real.

One of the main uses of fantasy, Tolkien says, in "On Fairy-Stories", is "recovery", the ability to see the natural world more clearly by dipping it in myth and strangeness—like Chesterton's story (that he never wrote) of the English yachtsman who lost his way in a fog and discovered England,

thinking it was a wild, faraway island with the most unbeliev-
ably exotic inhabitants and habits.

Chesterton wrote:

> The fairy-tale philosopher is glad that the leaf is green
> precisely because it might have been scarlet. He feels as if
> it had turned green an instant before he looked at it. He is
> pleased that snow is white on the strictly reasonable
> ground that it might have been black. Every colour has in
> it a bold quality as of choice; the red of garden roses is not
> only decisive but dramatic, like suddenly spilt blood.[1]

Tolkien probably had this passage in mind, at least unconsciously, when he wrote,

> [W]e need recovery. We should look at green again, and
> be startled anew (but not blinded) by blue and yellow and
> red. . . . Recovery . . . is a re-gaining—regaining of a clear
> view . . . "seeing things as we are (or were) meant to see
> them"—as things apart from ourselves. . . . We need
> . . . to clean our windows; so that the things seen clearly
> may be freed from the drab blur of triteness. . . . This
> triteness is really the penalty of "appropriation": . . . we
> laid hands on them, and then locked them in our hoard,
> acquired them, and acquiring, ceased to look at them
> ("On Fairy-Stories", pp. 57–58).

In other words, we need to return to the classical priority of
contemplation over action.

"Recovery" of a clear view of nature (the cosmos) is one
of the primary purposes of fantasy, according to Tolkien:

> Fantasy is made out of the Primary World, but a good
> craftsman loves his material. . . . By the forging of Gram
> cold iron was revealed; by the making of Pegasus horses
> were ennobled. . . .

[1] G. K. Chesterton, *Orthodoxy* (San Francisco: Ignatius Press, 1995) p. 64.

It was in fairy-stories that I first divined the potency of words, and the wonder of the things, such as stone, and wood, and iron; tree and grass; house and fire; bread and wine (ibid., p. 59).

There is a point Tolkien makes later in "On Fairy-Stories" that may seem to be a point about epistemology, or theory of knowledge (see chap. 6), but it is really a point about cosmology. It is the point that although fantasy is creative, it is also realistic; its truth conforms to the real world rather than (re-)creating it. It is therefore a rational activity, in the ancient, deeper, more basic meaning of "rational" (knowing reality). (We tend to mean by "rational" only "logical".) Since fantasy is rational, and since the cosmos is really full, fantasy too is full. Fantasy is a flight *to* reality.

> The keener and the clearer is the reason, the better fantasy will it make. If men were ever in a state in which they did not want to know or could not perceive truth (facts or evidence), then Fantasy would languish until they were cured. . . .
> For creative Fantasy is founded upon the hard recognition that things are so in the world as it appears under the sun; on a recognition of fact, but not a slavery to it. . . . If men really could not distinguish between frogs and men, fairy-stories about frog-kings would not have arisen (ibid., pp. 54–55).

One could even say that of the five aspects of a story—plot, characters, setting, style, and theme—it is the setting that is the most important in *The Lord of the Rings*. The real "hero" of *The Lord of the Rings* is Middle-earth itself! There are many detailed descriptions of topography that Tolkien learned to love on his many walking tours with the Inklings. This is why the maps are so important. Tolkien says, "I wisely started with a map, and made the story fit. . . . The other way about lands one in confusions . . . it is weary work to compose a map from a story" (*Letters*, no. 144, p. 177).

As the Elves are central in *The Silmarillion*, Hobbits are central in *The Lord of the Rings*: thus the greater importance of the natural setting in *The Lord of the Rings*. For Hobbits are far closer to nature than Elves or Men. They even live in the earth, in holes, a natural symbol for the depth of their earthiness.

Elves, though more transcendent to material nature than Men, are at the same time closer to it.

The Ents are the closest of all to nature. In fact, Tolkien makes nature itself live in the Ents. In Tolkien's world, *nothing* in nature is dead but all is alive, so much so that modern readers will call this cosmos "magical". A better word is "biblical". In Tolkien's cosmology, the earth as well as the heavens is not dumb but declares the glory of God.

C. S. Lewis had the same appreciation of nature's beauty and potency to reveal her Creator: "Any patch of sunlight in a wood will show you something about the sun which you could never get from reading books on astronomy. These pure and spontaneous pleasures are 'patches of Godlight' in the woods of our experience" (*Letters to Malcolm*, p. 91).

4.2 Do things have personalities?

The things in Tolkien's cosmos are not only beautiful; they also have something like personalities. The division between things and persons is not as absolute there as it is in our culture. Yet neither things nor persons are thereby demeaned, as modern materialism demeans persons and modern subjectivism demeans material things.

Ever since Descartes, the Western mind has separated

matter and spirit, body and soul, physical and spiritual, as two "clear and distinct ideas" that have nothing in common. Matter takes up space and does not think; mind thinks and does not take up space. But before Descartes it was not so. The distinction was there, but not total. There was an in-between category, *life*, which Descartes eliminated. (He thought of even an animal as a complicated machine.)

But Tolkien restores the ancient, pre-Cartesian cosmology in which things are not that neat. Even inorganic things like mountains are alive; the distinction between trees and Ents (thinking, treelike tree herders) is not absolute; and in general the whole world of things is more personlike, mindlike, spiritlike, than in the Cartesian machine-universe.

There are at least three killers of this old cosmology in the modern mind. One of them, of course, is materialism. Another is Cartesian dualism, which sells out half the world—everything made of matter—to materialism, reducing everything except mind and spirit to passivity and mechanism. The third is spiritualism, and the Gnostic New Age philosophy of "Create your own reality." Both materialism and spiritualism are attractive because they are simple. They are reductionisms. They obey Ockham's Razor ("Entities should not be multiplied beyond necessity"), as William of Ockham, a fourteenth-century English philosopher, formulated it—in other words, always use the simplest explanation. Modern science has found the Razor to be a very useful principle of method, but it does not follow that it is also a good principle of cosmology. It is true that reductionism (reducing the complex to the simple) is almost by definition the ideal of scientific explanation. The rules of grammar, chemical formulae, and road maps are examples. But to think that reality contains nothing more than the scientific method can know is like thinking that Shakespeare's plays are nothing but exercises in grammar, that the water that endlessly fascinates the poet and the mystic is actually nothing but hydrogen and oxygen, or that the road we actually travel has nothing more on it than the map does.

Part of the confusion comes from reducing Aristotle's four causes to one or, at the most, two. (1) Science can deal with the efficient cause (the agent of change). (2) It would seem that science can also deal with the material cause (what a thing is made of, the raw material or potentiality, that out of which something comes to be); but even this is not so, for "potentiality" is a metaphysical notion that dropped out of modern science with Descartes and Hobbes. (3) Science has definitely dropped the formal cause, the essence, the natural or metaphysical species (as distinct from humanly, conventionally arranged classes or categories). (4) And science has very self-consciously dropped final causality, purpose, teleology, design. That is the philosophical issue underlying the current dispute about evolution by blind accident versus evolution by cosmic design. Atheists resist the very idea of design in nature, because they see where it naturally (designedly?) leads: to a Designer of Nature.

A simple and startling example of how reductionistic we are can be found in C. S. Lewis's Narnia chronicles, from *The Voyage of the "Dawn Treader"*. I think we can learn much about ourselves from our reaction to this passage. We are willing to grant much "suspension of disbelief" in fantasy, especially when it describes another world; but notice how we rise up in protest against the apparent silliness of the idea presented here at first, and then how, upon reflection, we see the silliness not of the idea but of our prejudice:

"Are we near the World's End now, Sir?" asked Caspian.
"Have you any knowledge of the seas and lands farther east than this?"

"I saw them long ago," said the Old Man, "but it was from a great height. I cannot tell you such things as sailors need to know."

"Do you mean you were flying in the air?" Eustace blurted out.

"I was a long way above the air, my son," replied the Old Man. "I am Ramandu. But I see that you stare at one another and have not heard this name. And no wonder, for the days when I was a star had ceased long before any of you knew this world, and all the constellations have changed."

"Golly," said Edmund under his breath. "He's a *retired* star." . . .

"In our world," said Eustace, "a star is a huge ball of flaming gas."

"Even in your world, my son, that is not what a star is but only what it is made of." [2]

Lewis inserts Merlin into the plot in *That Hideous Strength* precisely to make the point that there was once more room in the cosmos for things of that sort.[3]

4.3 Is there real magic?

In Tolkien's cosmology, as in all pre-modern cosmologies, everything is more *alive*. Where the modern cosmology reduces the life of a dog to the life of a complex machine, Tolkien's cosmology expands the life of a mountain ("cruel Caradharas") to something like the life of an animal. Nothing is mere matter. Nothing is "mere" anything. Reduction-

---

[2] C. S. Lewis, *The Voyage of the "Dawn Treader"*, (New York: MacMillan, 1952), pp. 174–75.

[3] C. S. Lewis, *That Hideous Strength* (New York: Macmillan, 1952), see pp. 284–86.

ism is repudiated. More than that: there is so much life in things that we would call it "magic". Magic is potency, and power. But there are two very different kinds of magic—and here is one of the absolutely primary purposes of Tolkien's entire authorship. The two magics are not just different but opposed. In fact they are at war, and our civilization is in crisis because of the war between these two kinds of magic. One kind of magic, Enchantment, is our healing, and the other—the kind exemplified by the Ring—is our destruction.

The closest Tolkien ever comes to defining Faerie is "magic": "Faërie itself may perhaps most nearly be translated by Magic—but it is magic of a peculiar mood and power, at the furthest pole from the vulgar devices of the laborious, scientific, magician" ("On Fairy-Stories", p. 10). There are the two magics in a single sentence. The magic of Enchantment means entering the holy city of beauty, truth, and goodness and letting it conquer you. Ultimately, it means letting *God* conquer you, since beauty, truth, and goodness are divine attributes; they are what God is. But the magic of the "laborious, scientific magician" (that is, technology or, rather, the philosophy that makes "Man's conquest of Nature" by technology the *summum bonum*) means playing God, like Sauron. It is

a magic of external plans or devices (apparatus) instead of development of the inherent inner powers or talents . . . bulldozing the real world, or coercing other wills. The Machine is our more obvious modern form. . . . I have not used "magic" consistently, and indeed the Elven-queen Galadriel is obliged to remonstrate with the Hobbits on their confused use of the word both for the devices and operations of the Enemy, and for those of the Elves . . . the Elves are there [in my tales] to demonstrate the difference.

Their "magic" is Art. . . . And its object is Art not Power, sub-creation, not domination and tyrannous re-forming of Creation (*Letters*, no. 131, p. 146).

Faerian magic is the opposite of reductionism: it is creativity. It makes the world richer, it glorifies the world for beauty, it amplifies nature into art. The other magic destroys nature, reduces the world to a machine for the sake of power.

And the central symbol of *The Lord of the Rings*, the Ring, is precisely this second magic.

Both magics have potency. Faerian magic has internal or spiritual potency, the thing the Chinese call *te*, the power over the free human spirit of the good, the true, and the beautiful. *Te* is the right that makes its own might. The other magic, manifested in both technologism and totalitarianism, has external potency, power over bodies, coercive force. It is the might that makes its own right. The conflict between these two magics, these two relationships between might and right, is the central drama of the most famous work of philosophy ever written, Plato's *Republic*. ("It's all in Plato, all in Plato: bless me, what *do* they teach them at these schools!"—*The Last Battle*, p. 161.)

Here is the most direct sentence Tolkien ever wrote about the philosophy of *The Lord of the Rings*: "If I were to 'philosophize' this myth, or at least the Ring of Sauron, I should say it was a mythical way of representing the truth that *potency* . . . has to be externalised and so as it were passes, to a greater or less degree, out of one's direct control" (*Letters*, no. 211, p. 279). Surely this explains why we feel *weaker* and smaller than our pre-modern ancestors even while our power over nature has vastly grown.

The two magics have a number of things in common. Both are natural to man. Both can be either good or (when misused) evil. Technology becomes evil when it is turned from a means to an end. Fantasy becomes evil when it is turned into a create-your-own-reality philosophy. The ability to distinguish between reality and fantasy, between objective and subjective reality, is the first mark of sanity, and the confusion of the two is the first and most basic mark of insanity.

The two magics have something else in common: they have a common origin in the power of abstraction that makes possible the invention of the adjective, as Tolkien explains in his essay "On Fairy-Stories":

> The human mind, endowed with the powers of generalization and abstraction, sees not only *green-grass*, discriminating it from other things (and finding it fair to look upon), but sees that it is *green* as well as being *grass*. But how powerful, how stimulating to the very faculty that produced it, was the invention of the adjective: no spell or incantation in Faërie is more potent. . . . The mind that thought of *light, heavy, grey, yellow, still, swift*, also conceived of magic that would make heavy things light and able to fly, turn grey lead into yellow gold, and the still rock into a swift water. If it could do the one, it could do the other; it inevitably did both. When we can take green from grass, blue from heaven, and red from blood, we have already an enchanter's power—upon one plane; and the desire to wield that power in the world external to our minds awakes ("On Fairy-Stories", p. 22).

But though the two magics are one in their origin, they are opposite in their end. Enchantment's end is the surrender, or submission, of the soul to the beauty of nature and art. Technology's end is the conquest of nature by power. And this can be seen in their opposite relationships to *time*.

Technological magic works immediately. It attempts to

reduce the gap between desire and satisfaction, to eliminate the "shadow" that falls between the potency and the act (to quote T. S. Eliot's "The Hollow Men"). But in attacking the shadow it plunges us deeper into the shadow because time becomes more and more important to us, and more problematic, as we become more technologized. For the chief effect upon our lives of all those millions of time-saving devices with which technology has enriched our lives has been to destroy leisure rather than to enhance it. No one has any time anymore.

But Enchantment makes time irrelevant. The Hobbits lose track of time in Tom Bombadil's house, as we do when we read *The Lord of the Rings*, or when we make love, or surf, or look at the stars.

Bad enough is the attempt to conquer nature and time by this magic. Worse still is the attempt to conquer the bodies, minds, and wills of other persons. The reason this is worse is that technology amplifies potencies, and there is little or no evil potency in nature, but much in fallen men. Technology removes the quarantine set by weakness around the disease of sin.

C. S. Lewis argued persuasively, in *The Abolition of Man*, that all technological power over nature is always necessarily power over man, that "man's conquest of nature" must always turn out upon analysis to be some men's conquest of other men using nature as an instrument. Lewis explained the danger of technological magic:

> There is something which unites magic and applied science while separating both from the "wisdom" of earlier ages. For the wise men of old the cardinal problem had been how to conform the soul to reality, and the solution had been knowledge, self-discipline, and virtue. For magic and applied science (technology) alike the problem is how

to subdue reality to the wishes of men; the solution is a technique.[4]

There, in a single sentence, is the central difference between our modern Western civilization and all others, all that came before it. Lewis goes on to say:

> If we compare the chief trumpeter of the new era (Bacon) with Marlowe's Faustus, the similarity is striking. You will read in some critics that Faustus has a thirst for knowledge. In reality, he hardly mentions it. It is not truth he wants from his devils, but gold and guns and girls. . . . Bacon condemns those who value knowledge as an end in itself. . . . The true object is to extend Man's power (ibid., p. 88).

And critics say Tolkien's fantasy is escapist, unrealistic, and irrelevant to modern social problems! The problem is exactly the opposite: it is far too relevant for the critic's comfort.

---

[4] C. S. Lewis, *The Abolition of Man* (New York: Macmillan Publishing, 1947, 1955), pp. 87–88.

5

Anthropology

The Greeks, who invented philosophy as well as half of all the other worthwhile human things in the world, clearly recognized that in this world so full of wonders, the most wonderful by far was man. Compare the famous speech to that effect in *Oedipus Rex* with the twenty-eighth chapter of Job, and you will see the source of these two great ancient civilizations, Greece and Israel.

"Know thyself" was the maxim adopted by Socrates. If the philosopher does not know himself, he does not know who it is that knows all the other things he knows.

Obviously, knowing the self is the first, most immediate kind of knowing. Yet it is also the hardest, because it is the most prone to self-deception by self-interest and rationalization, because we are too close to see ourselves clearly, and because we alone are subjects, knowers; how can we make that same reality an object, a thing known? Yet we must.

5.1 Is death good or bad?

What knowledge may not be able to do, nature does. Death makes us an object, an It. Death puts life into question. Death forces us to think, prods us to become wise, as nothing else does. The most quoted quotation of the most quoted man (besides Shakespeare) in English literature, Doctor

Johnson, reads: "When a man knows he is to be hanged in a fortnight, it concentrates his mind wonderfully." (Watch the movie *Dead Man Walking* with this point in mind, and you may see a serious argument *for* capital punishment.)

Of all physical evils, death is the worst, the final one, the sum of them all, the loss of all earthly goods. Yet it also is the *best* thing for us if it is the door to Heaven. Abolishing death by artificial immortality would make us all into rotten eggs. We are designed to hatch. And if our culture's new *summum bonum*, the "conquest of nature", is pushed to its apotheosis of the conquest of death, we will see stunning parallels between Sauron and ourselves. There is a natural connection between this point about death and the previous one about the two magics and the spiritual danger of technology. Death is nature's trump card. Until death is conquered, nature is not conquered. And that is the point we have reached now. We are on the brink of the last frontier, our Crack of Doom.

Readers are almost always surprised when they learn that Tolkien himself considered the fundamental theme of *The Lord of the Rings* to be death and immortality: "I do not think that even Power and Domination is the real center of my story. . . . The real theme for me is about something much more permanent and difficult: Death and Immortality" (*Letters*, no. 186, p. 246).

Richard Purtill comments wisely on this surprise:

This statement by the author of the story must be taken seriously, but it is surprising, and at first we are inclined to resist accepting it. Very few of the characters die in the story. There is little talk of death or immortality, and there is certainly no description of or reflection on a life after death. Once we start thinking along these lines, however, we can see that there is perhaps more emphasis on death than we thought at first: the Barrow-wights, the Dead

Aragorn leads from the Paths of the Dead, the dead Elves
and Men Frodo and Sam see in the Dead Marshes, and
even the Black Riders are all reminders of death. Boromir,
Denethor, Théoden, and Gollum all die in scenes important to the plot; Gandalf and Frodo both seem to have
died at key points in the action. Furthermore, some of the
important images in the story could be taken as death
images: the blasted land of Mordor, the destruction of the
Ring, the passage over the Western Sea.

About immortality, however, Tolkien at first seems to
have almost nothing to say. . . . But . . . Tolkien is a writer
who achieves many of his most important effects by indi-
rection, and what is most important to him is often not
stated but underlies the whole story. As he says of religion,
"the religious element is absorbed into the story and the
symbolism".[1]

If the reader at first does not realize the centrality of death
to the story, and then later, upon reflection, does, Tolkien
himself seems to have gone through the same two stages of
awareness. He writes that "it is only in reading the work
myself . . . that I become aware of the dominance of the
theme of Death" (*Letters*, no. 208, p. 267). Aware not only of
death but of immortality, and the contrast between true and
false immortality, "the hideous peril of confusing true 'immortality' with limitless serial longevity" (ibid.).

Like the two magics, the two immortalities are opposites.
With false immortality, as life's quantity approaches infinity
its quality approaches zero. Gandalf explains, "A mortal,
Frodo, who keeps one of the Great Rings does not die, but
he does not grow or obtain more life, he merely continues
until at last every minute is a weariness. . . . He *fades*. . . .

[1] Richard L. Purtill, *J. R. R. Tolkien: Myth, Morality and Religion* (San Francisco: Ignatius Press, 2003), pp. 175–76.

Sooner or later the dark power will devour him" (LOTR, p. 46). In another letter, Tolkien explicitly connects this point with the one about the two magics: "To attempt by device or 'magic' to recover longevity is thus a supreme folly and wickedness for 'mortals.' Longevity or counterfeit 'immortality' . . . is the chief bait of Sauron—it leads the small to a Gollum, and the great to a Ringwraith" (*Letters*, no. 212, p. 286).

However, Tolkien does not condemn the desire for true immortality, an immortality consonant with our nature and our destiny as designed by a wise divine providence, as distinct from the depraved desire for a false and unnatural immortality under our own foolish control. In "On Fairy-Stories" he says that the highest purpose of fantasy, or the fairy tale, is the satisfaction of deep desires, and most especially the desire for immortality, "the oldest and deepest desire, the Great Escape: the Escape from Death. . . . Almost I would venture to assert that all complete fairy-stories must have it. . . . The *eucatastrophic* tale is the true form of fairy-tale, and its highest function" (pp. 67–68).

The "good catastrophe" is clear in "Leaf by Niggle", a fairy tale about death. Niggle's train journey is so obviously one of death that it is impossible not to see the story as an allegory. And the eucatastrophe is clearly true immortality, or Heaven, attained through self-giving, self-abnegation, and purgation—in fact, not a bad description of the "moral lesson" of *The Lord of the Rings*. This moral truth is not as simple, as clear, or as allegorical in *The Lord of the Rings* as it is in "Leaf by Niggle", but that does not mean that it is not present.

Two opposite kinds of death are required to attain the two opposite kinds of immortality. The false immortality requires the death of conscience. The real immortality requires the death of egotism. We can see this most clearly on the Hobbit level, in the contrast between Frodo and Gollum. Both physically die: Gollum at the Crack of Doom, Frodo by taking ship at the Grey Havens. But Gollum has died to his conscience, his soul, for the sake of his ego's craving for the Ring. Frodo has renounced possession of the Ring, and thus of his ego (for that is the Ring's power over him; that is why it has no power over Tom Bombadil). At the Crack of Doom it is not Frodo who falls into the fire of Hell but Gollum, the incarnation of Frodo's false self, the ego that craves the false immortality of power over everything, even death.

We could call this theme "good death versus bad death", death of the self (ego) versus death of the soul. It is also a central theme of one of the greatest books of the nineteenth century: *The Brothers Karamazov.* Dostoyevski insisted that John 12:24 ("Unless a grain of wheat falls into the earth and dies, it remains alone; but if it dies, it bears much fruit") be placed before his story, and he quoted it twice within the story. The point is not simply "Don't be egotistical, be unselfish." It is much more mysterious and wonderful than that. It is that he who voluntarily loses his life, gives up his life, for others, *will save it,* and he who chooses to cling to his life will lose it. When we try to be the lords of our own life, the life we cling to as our own is a miserable shadow of the true life that the true Lord wants to give us. But that life is so large and inconceivable that we cannot receive it unless our hands and minds are open, unless we give up our toys, our egos, our Rings.

Clearly this is the strange, surprising, even scandalous Christian vision of immortality: the road to immortality is the death of the ego. The pre-Christian classical world could conceive immortality only in an Olympian way, as an eter-nalizing of our natural human life and desires, not qualita-

tively transformed but only quantitatively amplified by unlimited longevity and power. Our culture still lives by three
dreams of immortality from paganism, only one of which is
consonant with Christianity. One dream is the ancient longing to become gods by moral heroism, like Oedipus. Another is the longing to become like gods by cleverness, like
Odysseus. (The modern version of cleverness is science and
technology.) The third is the Christian promise of immortality by the drowning of baptism, by being born again in blood
and water from the Cross.

Sigmund Freud was a famous and influential critic of the
Christian dream, but even he admits the failure of the pagan
one. In *Civilization and Its Discontents*, he lays out this puzzle:
(1) all men desire happiness; (2) all gods are only dreams born
of wishful thinking; (3) modern man has left his gods behind
because he has become a god himself, having fulfilled in his
own person, and by his own scientific cleverness and technological power, the ancient dreams that gave birth to the fairy-
tale fantasies of religion; yet (4) modern man is not happier
than ancient man. In fact, he is probably unhappier. And
Freud does not know why.

Tolkien's heroes are crypto-Christians. They do not know,
believe, mention, wonder about, or allegorize Christian doctrine. But they exemplify exactly what life would be like if
the Christian claims are true, especially its central paradox
about immortality through death and resurrection of the self,
self-realization through self-sacrifice. Frodo gives himself up
for the Shire, and for all Middle-earth, by accepting the
burden of the Ring and not lusting after it. It is this death,
this self-abnegation, that is precisely the central point about
death that Tolkien is making. It is not just Frodo's courage
and suffering, the inner torment of Frodo's soul ascending
Mount Doom; that is part of pagan wisdom too. It is not just

Frodo's incurable sadness and his inability to enjoy the Shire that he is left with afterward; that too is part of pagan tragic wisdom. Nor is it just the sad necessity for Frodo to take ship from Middle-earth forever at the end: that too is simply the pagan wisdom of "know-thyself" mortality. Those are all images of what Kierkegaard calls "the knight of infinite resignation" rather than "the knight of faith". Rather, in *The Lord of the Rings* we find the uniquely Christian kind of death, the mystical power of self-abnegation and self-donation, which makes full sense only as a consequence of Christ's death, as our incorporation into *that*. For Tolkien believes that "the greatest examples of the action of the spirit and of reason are in *abnegation*" (*Letters*, no. 186, p. 246). If this is not so, Jesus Christ was not the greatest man who ever lived but a failure and a fool. And so are all His followers, especially the saints.

Here is how C. S. Lewis explains the Christian view of death that formed the depths of Tolkien's soul from which *The Lord of the Rings* grew:

> Christian doctrine, if accepted, involves a particular view of Death. There are two attitudes towards Death which the human mind naturally adopts. One is the lofty view, which reached its greatest intensity among the Stoics, that Death "doesn't matter" . . . and that we ought to regard it with indifference (*Miracles*, p. 125).

Lewis demolishes this view from his own experience of his wife's death:

> It is hard to have patience with people who say "there is no death" or "Death doesn't matter." . . . You might as well say that birth doesn't matter. I look up at the night sky. Is anything more certain than that in all those vast times and spaces, if I were allowed to search them, I

should nowhere find her face, her voice, her touch? She died. She is dead. Is the word so difficult to learn? (*A Grief Observed*, p. 16).

The other [non-Christian view of death] is the "natural" point of view, implicit in nearly all private conversations on the subject . . . that Death is the greatest of all evils. . . . The first idea simply negates, the second simply affirms, our instinct for self-preservation. . . . Christianity countenances neither. Its doctrine is subtler. On the one hand Death is the triumph of Satan, the punishment of the Fall, and the last enemy. Christ shed tears at the grave of Lazarus and sweated blood in Gethsemane: the Life of Lives that was in Him detested this penal obscenity not less than we do, but more. On the other hand, only he who loses his life will save it. We are baptized into the *death* of Christ, and it is the remedy for the Fall. Death is, in fact, what some modern people call "ambivalent." It is Satan's great weapon and also God's great weapon; it is holy and unholy; our supreme disgrace and our only hope; the thing Christ came to conquer and the means by which He conquered (*Miracles*, p. 125).

Hence as suicide is the typical expression of the stoic spirit, and battle of the warrior spirit, martyrdom always remains the supreme enacting and perfection of Christianity.[2]

5.2 Is romance more thrilling than sex?

The Lord of the Rings is a touchstone for many things. One of those things is romance, or, rather, the relation between romance and sex.

The sexual revolution is one of the two things that most

[2] C. S. Lewis, *The Problem of Pain* (New York: Macmillan, 1978), p. 102.

radically, even spectacularly, distinguish our culture from all that went before it. The other is, of course, technology. The spiritual danger of technology is an obvious theme in *The Lord of the Rings*. But to some critics the other seems glaringly absent.

Edwin Muir wrote in *The Observer*: "All the characters are boys masquerading as adult heroes . . . and will never come to puberty. . . . Hardly one of them knows anything about women" (November 27, 1955). Does Muir's remark tell us something remarkable about Tolkien or about Muir and his culture? The best selling lampoon of *The Lord of the Rings*, *Bored of the Rings*, is about nothing but sex from cover to cover. Do we see an obsession here?

Suppose you read a book review complaining about the absence of missionaries, churches, and conversions in Julius Caesar's *The Conquest of Gaul*. Would this not imply that the critic was a very narrow-minded Fundamentalist and obsessed with his religion? Why should we draw a different conclusion when the critic's religious obsession is two feet lower down in the anatomy?

One could defend the absence of sex in *The Lord of the Rings* by blaming the Ring. Only when it is destroyed can life be normalized, and Men and Hobbits can love, marry, and procreate. None who have borne the Ring (except Sam) ever marry. But there is a deeper defense than this for the absence of sex in *The Lord of the Rings*: *The Lord of the Rings* not only is *about* a pre-Freudian culture but also was written by a man of a pre-Freudian culture.

The fact that *The Lord of the Rings*' natural gravity is not drawn to sex as its center simply means that it does not come from our culture, just as the fact that the *Odyssey* does not mention mystical experience simply means that it did not come from Hindu culture.

But sex—or rather, romantic love—is there, indeed, though it is not usually noticed. Purtill noticed it:

> We have the heroic love of Aragorn for Arwen . . . and the homely, domestic love of Sam Gamgee and Rosie Cotton. Somewhere in between is the love story of Eowyn, daughter of King Theoden. She begins with a romantic, unrealistic love for Aragorn, who has loved Arwen for centuries. (He is of long-lived human-Elvish stock, and Arwen can choose either Elvish immortality or mortality with her human lover.) Eventually Eowyn finds happiness with Faramir, son of Denethor (Purtill, *J. R. R. Tolkien*, p. 105).

How many romances would be enough for the central characters, if not three?

Peter Jackson expanded on the Aragorn-Arwen romance in the movie, and this was quite in character, not only in spirit but literally, for, as Tolkien himself writes, "The romance between Aragorn and Arwen, Elrond's daughter, is only alluded to as a known thing. It is told elsewhere in a short tale, *Of Aragorn and Arwen Undomiel*. I think the simple 'rustic' love of Sam and his Rosie (nowhere elaborated) is *absolutely essential* to . . . the theme of the relation of ordinary life (breathing, eating, working, begetting) and quests, sacrifice, causes, and the 'longing for Elves', and sheer beauty" (*Letters*, no. 131, p. 161). Sex and romance receive the same treatment as other aspects of life in *The Lord of the Rings*, as examples of the interdependency between the high (Aragorn) and the low (Sam).

Here is Tolkien's philosophy of sex, romance, love, and marriage presented as directly as anyone could wish, in a letter to his son Michael:

> The romantic chivalric tradition . . . can be very good, since it takes . . . fidelity, and so self-denial, "service,"

courtesy, honour, and courage. Its weakness is, of course, that . . . its centre was not God, but imaginary Deities, Love and the Lady. . . . This is, of course, false and at best make-believe. . . . It takes the young man's eye off women as they are, as companions in shipwreck not guiding stars. (One result is the observation of the actual to make the young man turn cynical.) . . . It inculcates exaggerated notions of "true love," as a fire from without, a permanent exaltation, unrelated to age, childbearing, and plain life, and unrelated to will and purpose. (One result of that is to make young folk look for a "love" that will keep them always nice and warm in a cold world, without any effort of theirs; and the incurably romantic go on looking even in the squalor of the divorce courts.) . . .

Only the rarest good fortune brings together the man and woman who are really as it were "destined" for one another, and capable of a very great and splendid love. The idea still dazzles us, catches us by the throat: poems and stories in multitudes have been written on the theme, more, probably, than the total of such loves in real life. . . . In such great inevitable love, often love at first sight, we catch a vision, I suppose, of marriage as it should have been in an unfallen world (*Letters*, no. 43, pp. 48–49, 52).

But, as C. S. Lewis explains in *The Four Loves*, this is an illusion.

The grim joke is that this Eros whose voice seems to speak from the eternal realm is not himself necessarily even permanent. He is notoriously the most mortal of our loves. The world rings with complaints of his fickleness. What is baffling is the combination of this fickleness with his protestations of permanency. To be in love is both to intend and to promise lifelong fidelity. Love makes vows unasked; can't be deterred from making them. "I will be ever true," are almost the first words he utters. Not hypocritically but sincerely. No experience will cure him of the delusion. We have all heard of people who are in love again every few years; each time sincerely convinced that *"this* time it's the real thing," that their wanderings are over, that they have found their true love and will themselves be true till death.

And yet Eros is in a sense right to make this promise. The event of falling in love is of such a nature that we are right to reject as intolerable the idea that it should be transitory. In one high bound it has overleaped the massive wall of our selfhood; it has made appetite itself altruistic, tossed personal happiness aside as a triviality and planted the interests of another in the centre of our being. Spontaneously and without effort we have fulfilled the law (towards one person) by loving our neighbour as ourselves. It is an image, a foretaste, of what we must become to all if Love Himself rules in us without a rival. It is even (well used) a preparation for that. Simply to relapse from it, merely to "fall out of" love again, is—if I may coin the ugly word, a sort of *disredemption.* Eros is driven to promise what Eros of himself cannot perform. . . . Eros, having made his gigantic promise and shown you in glimpses what its performance would be like, has "done his stuff." He, like a godparent, makes the vows; it is we who must keep them. . . . We must do the works of Eros when Eros is not present.[3]

Another aspect of sex and romance that is often criticized in Tolkien is his supposed gender stereotyping. His men are true men, his women are true women, there is no homosexuality, and no confusion of sexual identities or even roles—except on the part of Eowyn, who willfully demands to be a Joan of Arc type warrior instead of obeying her

[3] C. S. Lewis, *The Four Loves* (London: Collins Fontana, 1960), pp. 104–5.

king's command to stay home and care for the women and children:

> "Let me ride in your following. For I am weary of skulking in the hills, and wish to face peril and battle."
> "Your duty is with your people," he answered.
> "Too often have I heard of duty," she cried. "But am I not of the House of Eorl, a shieldmaiden and not a dry-nurse? I have waited on faltering feet long enough. Since they falter no longer, it seems, may I not now spend my life as I will?"
> "Few may do that with honour," he answered. "But as for you, lady: did you not accept the charge to govern the people until their lord's return? . . ."
> "All your words are but to say: you are a woman, and your part is in the house. . . . But I am of the House of Eorl and not a serving-woman. I can ride and wield blade, and I do not fear either pain or death."
> "What do you fear, lady?" he asked.
> "A cage," she said (LOTR, p. 767).

Tolkien has double sympathies here, for on the one hand the words spoken to her here by Aragorn are true, and Eowyn's disobedience is nearly punished with death (but for the intervention of Merry). But it is eventually rewarded by a grace, not a justice: it is Eowyn, disguised as the soldier Dernhelm, who slays the Lord of the Nazgul.

Eowyn is a Joan of Arc figure, but remember that Joan of Arc is very different from a modern feminist. Like Eowyn, she transcended social gender roles, but she did not question those roles themselves, like a modern feminist. Like her society, and like all pre-modern societies, including those in *The Lord of the Rings*, she accepted those roles as archetypes, not stereotypes. Archetypes are natural (or Platonically su-pernatural) and help construct our identity; stereotypes are unnatural, and thwart it. Archetypes are discovered by the sage; stereotypes are invented by the propagandist. Archetypes are utterly and eternally rational; stereotypes are irrational. Roles change, archetypes do not. And roles are judged by archetypes, not vice versa.

C. S. Lewis presents the old archetypes of masculinity and femininity that are embedded in the pre-modern mind and in Tolkien's in a vision at the end of *Perelandra*. The protagonist, Ransom (who coincidentally was modeled on Tolkien), sees the archetypes of Masculine and Feminine, Yang and Yin, Mars and Venus, concretized and incarnated. The "Oyarsa" mentioned here are both angels (spirits) and archetypes (Platonic Forms, essences):

> The Oyarsa of Mars shone with cold and morning colours, a little metallic—pure, hard, and bracing. The Oyarsa of Venus glowed with a warm splendour, full of the suggestion of teeming vegetable life. . . .
> Malacandra [Mars] was like rhythm and Perelandra [Venus] like melody. Malacandra affected him like a quantitative, Perelandra like an accentual, metre. He thinks that the first held in his hands something like a spear, but the hands of the other were open, with the palms turned toward him. . . . The two white creatures were sexless. But he of Malacandra was masculine (not male); she of Perelandra was feminine (not female). Malacandra seemed to him to have the look of one standing armed, at the ramparts of his own remote archaic world, in ceaseless vigilance, his eyes ever roaming the east-ward horizon whence his danger came long ago. "A sailor's look," Ransom once said to me; "you know . . . eyes that are impregnated with distance." But the eyes of Perelandra opened, as it were, inward, as if they were the curtained gateway to a world of waves and murmurings and wandering airs, of life that rocked in winds and splashed on mossy stones and

descended as the dew and arose sunward in thin-spun delicacy of mist. On Mars the very forests are of stone; in Venus the lands swim. For now he thought of them no more as Malacandra and Perelandra. He called them by their Tellurian [earthly] names. With deep wonder he thought to himself, "My eyes have seen Mars and Venus. I have seen Ares and Aphrodite." [4]

5.3 Why do humans have identity crises?

This is one of the most remarkable themes in anthropology, and one that flabbergasts and discombobulates many people, rather like Plato's Theory of Ideas in metaphysics. The point is that the self is not a given, an object, whose essential nature is unchangeable. Triangles can never be non-triangular, and rocks are always guaranteed to be rocky, grass grassy, and dogs doggy—but humans can be inhuman. We alone can fail to achieve our nature. Our nature is a task to achieve, not a fact to receive.

The existentialist philosophers have emphasized this theme the most, and some (notably Sartre) have attached to it questionable corollaries: that we have no essence, or meaning, that life is therefore meaningless, that we must create our own values, that we are gods, and that all conformity and receptivity are threatening and dehumanizing to our freedom. But the point does not require any of those corollaries. It is quite traditional and is as old as Boethius's *Consolation of Philosophy*:

> Whatever is must also be [ontologically] good. And it follows from this that whatever loses its goodness ceases to

[4] C. S. Lewis, *Perelandra* (New York: Macmillan, 1944), pp. 198–200.

be. Thus wicked men cease to be what they were. . . . To give oneself to evil . . . is to lose one's human nature. Just as virtue can raise a person above human nature, so vice lowers those whom it has seduced from the condition of men beneath human nature. For this reason, anyone whom you find transformed by vice cannot be counted a man [or a Hobbit: Gollum is an ex-Hobbit, a failed Hobbit, as the Ringwraiths are ex-men, or 'Un-men', to use C. S. Lewis's chilling term from *Perelandra*]. . . . The man who is driven by avarice . . . is like a wolf; the restless, angry man who spends his life in quarrels you will compare to a dog. The treacherous conspirator who steals by fraud may be likened to a fox; the man who is ruled by intemperate anger is thought to have the soul of a lion. The fearful and timid man who trembles without reason is like a deer; the lazy, stupid fellow is like an ass. The volatile, inconstant man who continually changes direction is like a bird; the man who is sunk in foul lust is trapped in the pleasures of a filthy sow. In this way, anyone who abandons virtue ceases to be a man, since he cannot share in the divine nature, and instead becomes a beast.[5]

The theme we will explore in the next section is a much more familiar one in writers like C. S. Lewis, Augustine, and the Romantics: *Sehnsucht*, the mysterious longing for we-know-not-what, our lover's quarrel with the world, our innate desire for the transcendent, the perfect, the "more". Yet the foundation for this familiar theme of longing is the unfamiliar one of the elusiveness and volatility of the self. We cannot help desiring to be other than we are because we do not yet have our true being; we can gain it or lose it. Our very being is trembling, not stable. We can lose our selves. Nothing else can.

[5] Boethius, *Consolation of Philosophy*, trans. Richard Green (Indianapolis: Bobbs Merrill, 1962), bk. 4, pp. 82–83.

This innate desire, this reaching beyond ourselves, can lead us to our true selves and to God, our Author, as it led C. S. Lewis in *Surprised by Joy*. But it can also lead down darker paths of desire: idolatry and fetishism. When the object we desire is God, or that which God is (truth, goodness, and beauty), the object is not possessable. And paradoxically, only then are we fulfilled, when we do *not* possess the object we desire but it possesses us. But when we make anything other than God our object of desire, when our goal is possessable, we are undone. This dark path began in Eden. Once we laid hands on the fruit we desired, the horrible effect took place immediately: it laid its hands on us. The self was "unselfed"—not filled but emptied, not enhanced but devastated. The object grew into a god, and we shrank into slaves. We exchanged places: we became the objects, the its, and it became the subject, the I. We found our identity in what was less than ourselves, in what we could possess. We were possessed by our possession, or by our possessiveness. We who began as the Adam (Man) became the golem, the "Un-man".

Frodo and Sam illustrate one half of this paradox, Gollum the other. Frodo and Sam attain and save their selves because they give themselves away for others, for the world. And not for some abstract cause but for each other and for the Shire. In contrast, Gollum is obsessed with his "cause": possessing the Ring. His selfishness is so self-devouring that he almost has no self left. He talks to himself more than to others; he often makes no distinction between himself and his "Precious"; he is confused about who he is. He speaks of himself in the third person. ("Don't let them hurt us, Precious!") It is the Ring that is now the Precious, and Gollum has lost his preciousness, his value. He has become its slave, and it has become his master. In fact it has become the self, the person, the subject, the actor, and Gollum has become its passive object, its *IT*. He has placed his soul inside the fetish (as Sauron did when he made the Ring), so that without it his soul is literally torn in two. He is nothing without the Ring. He cannot distinguish himself from the Ring. He *is* the Ring. The person has become a thing. He has lost his soul.

When Sauron forged the Ring, he put into it some of his power, and therefore some of his identity, since power is what he identified with, or found his identity in. Thus for him, as for Gollum, to lose the Ring is to lose his self. And one who has lost his self, who has only emptiness and ashes for his self, will always demand to reduce all other selves to emptiness and ashes. This is why Sauron must reduce all Middle-earth to ashes: to *his* ashes, to himself.

And this is what we do whenever we "identify with" our *stuff*. George MacDonald says, "A man is enslaved to whatever he cannot part with that is less than himself" (Lewis, *George MacDonald: An Anthology*, no. 57, p. 26).

Sauron is uncomfortably familiar. He is only an exaggeration, a caricature, an enlargement of ourselves or, rather, of one possibility for ourselves. Down that road we find the Lieutenant of the Black Gate of Barad-dur: "His name is remembered in no tale; for he himself had forgotten it, and he said: 'I am the Mouth of Sauron'" (LOTR, p. 870).

This mysterious point about the volatility, or fragility, of selfhood, is put more clearly by C. S. Lewis in *Mere Christianity*:

> Every time you make a choice you are turning the central part of you, the part of you that chooses, into something a little different from what it was before. And taking your life as a whole, with all your innumerable choices, all your life long you are slowly turning this central thing either

into a heavenly creature or into a hellish creature; either
into a creature that is in harmony with God, and with
other creatures, and with itself, or else into one that is in a
state of war and hatred with God, and with its fellow-
creatures, and with itself. To be the one kind of creature is
heaven: that is, it is joy and peace and knowledge and
power. To be the other means madness, horror, idiocy,
rage, impotence, and eternal loneliness. Each of us at each
moment is progressing to the one state or the other (*Mere
Christianity*, pp. 86–87).

5.4 What do we most deeply desire?

Just as there are two opposite magics in *The Lord of the Rings*,
there are two opposite longings, or deep desires. There is, of
course, the desire to possess the Ring; and that corresponds
to the magic of power, and technology. More subtly and
sweetly, there is also another desire, a longing whose object
cannot be defined, much less possessed. This longing sweeps
through *The Lord of the Rings* like a wind over the sea. In fact,
the sea is one of its symbols, especially for Legolas (see LOTR,
p. 935), as it was for Tolkien and many island-dwelling
Englishmen.

Tolkien himself was haunted by a recurrent dream of the
sea. He speaks of

> my Atlantis-hunting. This legend or myth or dim
> memory of some ancient history has always troubled me.
> In sleep I had the dreadful dream of the ineluctable Wave,
> either coming out of the quiet sea, or coming in towering
> over the green islands. It still occurs occasionally, though
> now exorcized by writing about it. It always ends by
> surrender, and I awake gasping out of deep water (*Letters*,
> no. 257, p. 347).

Any mystic or any surfer would understand that. Of course it is not literally the sea, or the wave, but the thing they symbolize. And that is obviously God, and Heaven or Paradise, or union with God. It is no accident that when Lewis writes about an unfallen planetary Eden, it is an ocean planet of floating islands that must be ridden like waves.

There are literally hundreds of lines in *The Lord of the Rings* that express this longing for something lost, something Edenic. The past haunts the present like an undersea creature that constantly troubles the surface of the water. It is much more than mere nostalgia for "the good old days". It is also more than traditionalism's practical payoff of getting things that are useful for yourself by remembering what was useful for your ancestors. Rather, the past *as such* has a fascination. And this is not because of its content; for if we could return, we would not be fulfilled; we would not find Eden.

It is its very unattainability that makes the past such a powerful symbol of something that is unattainable not because it is past but because it is future, or, rather, transcendent to all history. What is achieved by the "haunting of history" in *The Lord of the Rings* is not nostalgia but *Sehnsucht*: a longing for the transcendent, the "more".

Already in the second chapter we see it in Frodo:

> Often he wandered by himself, and to the amazement of sensible folk he was sometimes seen far from home walking in the hills and woods under the starlight. Merry and Pippin suspected that he visited the Elves at times, as Bilbo had done. . . . He found himself wondering at times, especially in the autumn, about the wild lands, and strange visions of mountains that he had never seen came into his dreams. He . . . began to feel restless, and the old paths seemed too well-trodden. He looked at maps, and wondered what lay beyond their edges: maps made in the

Shire showed mostly white spaces beyond its borders
(LOTR, pp. 41–42).

It is not clear what is being desired here, but it is "something
more".

The "more" is qualitative, not quantitative. It is a desire for
a step up the hierarchy of being, for communion with more
exalted beings. It is, in fact, a desire for communion with
Elves: "Sam . . . believed he had once seen an Elf in the
wood, and still hoped to see more one day. Of all the legends
that he had heard in his early years such fragments of tales
and half-remembered stories about the Elves as the hobbits
knew, had always moved him most deeply" (LOTR, p. 44).

It is also a desire somehow to transcend ordinary time;
this is done in Elvish places: Rivendell and Lothlorien. Bilbo
says of Rivendell, "Time doesn't seem to pass here: it just is.
A remarkable place altogether" (LOTR, p. 225). And in
Lothlorien,

> Frodo felt that he was in a timeless land that did not fade
> or change or fall into forgetfulness. When he had gone
> and passed again into the outer world, still Frodo the
> wanderer from the Shire would walk there. Frodo stood
> still, hearing far off great seas upon beaches that had long
> ago been washed away, and sea-birds crying whose race
> had perished from the earth (LOTR, p. 342).

And we too—we readers who have walked into *The Lord of
the Rings* as Frodo has walked into Lothlorien—we feel like
Sam when he first meets the Elves in the Shire forests: "Sam
walked along at Frodo's side, as if in a dream, with an
expression on his face half of fear and half of astonished joy"
(LOTR, p. 80).

The sea, the stars, and the Elves seem to be the most
powerful catalysts for this desire, or images of its mysterious

object. The three are connected in the figure of Earendil, the mariner "from Otherworld beyond the Sea", who "came unto the timeless halls where shining fall the countless years" (LOTR, pp. 228–29) and is now revered as "Earendil, the Evening Star, most beloved of the elves" (LOTR, p. 355). It was this name, this single word in an eighth-century Anglo-Saxon poem "Crist", that first moved Tolkien to create his myth from which *The Lord of the Rings* grew.

The Elves themselves feel the sea-longing. Legolas confesses that "deep in the hearts of all my kindred lies the sea-longing, which it is perilous to stir. Alas! for the gulls. No peace shall I have again under beech or under elm" (LOTR, p. 855).

The sea is a nearly universal symbol of death. Thus Frodo, like King Arthur, or like a Viking hero, leaves Middle-earth forever *by ship*. There seems to be a fairly obvious connection between this sea love and the desire for something that can be attained only after death.

C. S. Lewis helps us to understand this desire as well as anyone ever has, I think. It is not mere boredom or discontent, for it comes not at the worst times but at the best—as Psyche explains to Orual in *Till We Have Faces:*

"I have always . . . had a kind of longing for death."

"Ah, Psyche," I said, "have I made you so little happy as that?"

"No, no, no," she said. "You don't understand. Not that kind of longing. It was when I was happiest that I longed most. It was on happy days when we were up there on the hills, the three of us, with the wind and the sunshine. . . . And because it was so beautiful, it set me longing, always longing. Somewhere else there must be more of it. Everything seemed to be saying, Psyche come! But I couldn't (not yet) come and I didn't know where

I was to come to. It almost hurt me. I felt like a bird in a cage." [6]

What *is* it then?

> It is distinguished from other longings by two things. In the first place, though the sense of want is acute and even painful, yet the mere wanting is felt to be somehow a delight. . . . This hunger is better than any other fullness; this poverty better than all other wealth. . . .
>
> In the second place, there is a peculiar mystery about the *object* of this desire. . . . Every one of these supposed objects for the Desire is inadequate to it. [7]

> It is from this point of view that we can understand hell in its aspect of privation. All your life an unattainable ecstasy has hovered just beyond the grasp of your consciousness. The day is coming when you will wake to find, beyond all hope, that you have attained it, or else, that it was within your reach and you have lost it forever (*The Problem of Pain*, p. 118).

Lewis then interprets this data as a kind of experiential proof of the existence of God: "This Desire was, in the soul, as the Siege Perilous in Arthur's castle—the chair in which only one could sit. And if nature makes nothing in vain, the One who can sit in this chair must exist" (*Pilgrim's Regress*, p. 10).

> Creatures are not born with desires unless satisfaction for those desires exists. A baby feels hunger: well, there is such a thing as food. A duckling wants to swim: Well, there is such a thing as water. Men feel sexual desire: well, there is such a thing as sex. If I find in myself a desire

[6] C. S. Lewis, *Till We Have Faces* (New York: Harcourt, Brace, 1956), p. 74.

[7] C. S. Lewis, *The Pilgrim's Regress* (Grand Rapids, Mich.: Eerdmans, 1981), pp. 7–8.

which no experience in this world can satisfy, the most probable explanation is that I was made for another world (Lewis, *Mere Christianity*, p. 120).

If you are really a product of a materialistic universe, how is it you don't feel at home there? Do fish complain of the sea for being wet? Or if they did, would that fact itself not strongly suggest that they had not always been, or would not always be, purely aquatic creatures? Notice how we are perpetually *surprised* at Time. ("How time flies! Fancy John being grown-up and married! I can hardly believe it!") In heaven's name, why? Unless, indeed, there is something in us which is *not* temporal.[8]

Tolkien, of course, does not give us these Christian interpretations or arguments in *The Lord of the Rings*. But that is not because *The Lord of the Rings* is not Christian, but because it is not interpretation and argument. It is fiction.

But did Tolkien deliberately intend that *The Lord of the Rings* should have this *effect* on us? Of course he did. For in "On Fairy-Stories" he explicitly points to this arousal of desire as fantasy's primary end.

But desire for what? In "On Fairy-Stories" Tolkien mentions four aspects of this desire that fairy tales both stimulate and satisfy: fantasy, recovery, escape, and consolation. In one word, it is Paradise. We live in a fallen, broken world. And we remember and long for another. That is why "this world is not enough", why we have our "lover's quarrel with the world". To use Pascal's image, we are like disinherited princes: if we did not remember our kingly other-worldly glory, why would we be so dissatisfied with this beautiful world? But we are, even (especially!) when it is at its best: in sunsets and stars and storms and symphonies.

[8] Letter to Sheldon Vanauken, quoted in Sheldon Vanauken, *A Severe Mercy* (San Francisco: Harper and Row, 1977), p. 93.

We feel as if we are in the middle of the classic Vermont farmer joke: "You can't get there from here." Then how . . . ? Only the Incarnation brings Heaven back to earth. Only Christ fulfills this universal longing. Very subtly, yet very deeply, *The Lord of the Rings* really points to Christ. That is why its central symbol is the Ring: it is the exact opposite of the Cross (see chap. 14).

6

Epistemology

Epistemology is that division of philosophy which studies knowledge—not the objects of knowledge, or the content of knowledge, but knowledge itself, how we know, and whether we can attain truth, and if so how. There are many words for "knowledge" in Greek; "epistemology" comes from *episteme*, which means "certain knowledge".

Epistemology is important because it makes a great difference what kind of knowing we can trust, if any. Can *any* knowledge be trusted, or must we begin and end with scepticism? Descartes only began with scepticism, as a method (his "universal methodic doubt"); a sceptic ends with it as his final verdict on human knowledge.

If there is some kind of reliable knowledge, and we do not have to be sceptics, the next question is how we attain it: by reason (rationalism) or sensation (empiricism), or both (realism) or neither (mysticism)? Is it immediate and intuitive, or by proof and argument, whether deductive or inductive?

Perhaps the most practical question in epistemology is: What sources of knowledge can we trust? Ancient traditions? Intuition? People? Which ones? How do we recognize trustworthy people? Do we have a *third eye*, an eye of the heart, in addition to the eyes on the outside of the head and the eye of the brain on the inside of the head? Does the heart *know* as well as feel and desire? Does the heart have reasons that the reason cannot know?

On many occasions in *The Lord of the Rings* the Fellowship, especially Frodo and Sam, have to make choices that are not merely moral choices between known good and known evil, but epistemological choices between wisdom and folly, reality and appearance, in choosing between two apparent goods or two apparent evils, especially what to do with the Ring.

The question of whom to trust frequently arises. For instance, how did Frodo know "Strider" was trustworthy when he first met him at Bree? He "feels fair and seems foul"—is this "feeling" the eye of the heart and the "seeming" the eye of the head?

How to know when to mete out justice and when to give mercy is another epistemological question, as well as a moral question. Neither Frodo nor even Gandalf knew the role Gollum was destined to play; yet Gandalf says, "My heart tells me he has some role to play yet, for good or ill, before the end" (LOTR, p. 58). How did Gandalf know this? He did not know the future; he was not a prophet. In the terms of *The Lion, the Witch and the Wardrobe*, he knew it because he knew "the Deeper Magic from Before the Dawn of Time".

6.1 Is knowledge always good?

It sounds scandalous to any rationalist, classical or modern, but sometimes it is "better not to know" (LOTR, p. 448). Sometimes knowing is dangerous. "Perilous to us all are the devices of an art deeper than we possess ourselves" (LOTR, p. 583). We can control the world but we cannot control our own control; and if we do not know ourselves, we will not know *that* truth.

Thus knowledge (as distinct from wisdom) cannot be the supreme good, for it is compatible with evil, just as power is.

Especially when the knowledge is only by analysis, by breaking the thing into parts. "He that breaks a thing in order to find out what it is has left the path of wisdom" (*Letters*, no. 346, p. 424). This is Gollum's path:

He was interested in roots and beginnings; he dived into deep pools; he burrowed under trees and growing plants; he tunneled into green mounds; and he ceased to look up at the hill-tops, or the leaves on trees, or the flowers opening in the air: his head and his eyes were downward. . . . [H]e used [the ring] to find out secrets, and he put his knowledge to crooked and malicious uses. . . . The ring had given him power according to his stature. . . . All the great "secrets" under the mountains had turned out to be just empty night: there was nothing more to find out, nothing worth doing (LOTR, pp. 51–52, 54).

One wonders how much of the above is a description of our own culture's Gollum-like exchange of ancient wisdom for modern knowledge. One also suspects that we all really know this, in our unconscious, for that is where language comes from, and our language does not say "modern wisdom".

The ranks of literary critics of fantasy are full of Gollums. Tolkien says of Faerie, "Its very richness and strangeness tie the tongue of a traveler who would report them. And while he is there it is dangerous for him to ask too many questions, lest the gates should be shut and the keys be lost" ("On Fairy-Stories", p. 33). "Faërie . . . has many ingredients, but analysis will not necessarily discover the secret of the whole" (ibid., p. 30).

Tolkien says, "As a story, I think it is good that there should be a lot of things unexplained (especially if an explanation actually exists). . . . There must be some enigmas, as there always are. Tom Bombadil is one (intentionally)" (*Letters*, no. 144, p. 174). Any good storyteller always suggests more than he says, or even knows, to give us the sense of a vast sea of wisdom underlying the story, and a sense of our own smallness, and these two senses together elicit wonder. Fantasy does this better than science fiction, because science fiction deals with the scientifically possible, thus with problems and puzzles that could in principle be solved and some day probably will, while fantasy deals with things beyond the capacity of natural science to explain or control.

Any theist could explain and justify the wisdom of ignorance. As C. S. Lewis put it, "[H]ow can the characters in a play guess the plot? We are not the playwright, we are not the producer, we are not even the audience. We are on the stage. To play well the scenes in which we are 'on' concerns us much more than to guess about the scenes that follow it." [1]

6.2 Is intuition a form of knowledge?

The central debate in classical modern philosophy is between the epistemologies of rationalism (Descartes, Spinoza, Leibniz, Hegel) and empiricism (Bacon, Hobbes, Locke, Hume). The issue is the priority of reason or sense experience.

Both epistemologies ignore a more ancient organ of knowing: intuition. Pascal appeals to this in his famous saying: "The heart has its reasons which reason knows nothing of." This is not a justification of sentiment, feeling, or desire over reason, but an expansion of the meaning of *reason* beyond "calculation" to "intuition".

[1] C. S. Lewis, *The World's Last Night and Other Essays* (New York: Harcourt, Brace, Jovanovitch, 1952, 1960), p. 104.

At least a dozen times during his quest Frodo chooses to follow his heart over his calculating reason and his experience, and most of the time the choice turns out to be crucially right. (See the Concordance for examples.) Tolkien's epistemology includes trust in this third eye of the heart. But the heart is not an infallible organ. (Remember the uncertainties in the chapter entitled "The Choices of Master Samwise".) Sauron's and Saruman's hearts and intuitions mislead them. For this "third eye", unlike reason and sense experience, depends on moral goodness; it is trustworthy only in the virtuous. So virtue is part of epistemology! Epistemology depends on ethics; knowledge (of the highest and most important things) depends on goodness. That's what Jesus said, after all: "My teaching is not mine, but his who sent me; if any man's will is to do his will, he shall know whether the teaching is from God" (Jn 7:16–17). And, "Blessed are the pure in heart, for they shall see God" (Mt 5:8).

We must be careful here. This is *not* "Get in touch with your own higher consciousness", "Listen to your feelings", or even "Feel the Force". Frodo is humble and knows he lacks the wisdom the Quest demands, so he listens to others, to his superiors, and to tradition. And when he has to rely on his own intuition, it is his moral innocence, not any epistemological or psychological method, that saves him.

Frodo learns from experience, but not the way Goethe's Faust does. He does not eat experience like a spider eating flies, trapping them in the web of his consciousness. He lets himself be tutored by experience because he believes in objective truth and, implicitly, in a providential order in the world. That's why he trusts experience. As C. S. Lewis put it, "What I like about experience is that it is such an honest thing. You may take any number of wrong turnings; but keep your eyes open and you will not be allowed to go very far before the warning signs appear. You may have deceived yourself, but experience is not trying to deceive you. The universe rings true wherever you fairly test it." [2]

Lewis explains *why* intuition sees more than literal sight or literal reason and scientific analysis in a profound little essay in epistemology called "Meditation in a Toolshed". What he means in the following passage by "looking along" is one form of intuition, or the "eye of the heart". It is the ancient and forgotten art of sign reading, seeing the things in the universe not as mere brute facts but as signs, as significant, as a kind of language, and thus as implicitly designed by a Mind. (It was a medieval cliché that "God wrote two books, nature and Scripture.")

> I was standing today in the dark toolshed. The sun was shining outside and through the crack at the top of the door there came a sunbeam. From where I stood that beam of light, with the specks of dust gyrating in it, was the most striking thing in the place. Everything else was almost pitch-black. I was seeing the beam, not seeing things by it.
>
> Then I moved, so that the beam fell on my eyes. Instantly the whole previous picture vanished. I saw no toolshed, and (above all) no beam. Instead I saw, framed in the irregular cranny at the top of the door, green leaves moving on the branches of a tree outside and beyond that, 90 odd million miles away, the sun. Looking along the beam, and looking at the beam are very different experiences.
>
> But this is only a very simple example of the difference between looking at and looking along. A young man

---

[2] C. S. Lewis, *Surprised by Joy* (New York: Harcourt, Brace, and World, 1955), p. 177.

meets a girl. The whole world looks different when he
sees her. . . . He is, as they say, "in love". Now comes a
scientist and describes this young man's experience from
the outside. For him it is all an affair of the young man's
genes and a recognized biological stimulus. That is the
difference between looking *along* the sexual impulse and
looking *at* it. . . .
   The people who look *at* things have had it all their own
way; the people who look *along* things have simply been
brow-beaten. . . . That, in fact, is the whole basis of the
specifically "modern" type of [reductionist] thought.[3]

In *The Abolition of Man* he applies this principle to moral
values:

   You cannot go on "explaining away" for ever: you will
   find that you have explained explanation itself away. You
   cannot go on "seeing through" things for ever. The whole
   point of seeing through something is to see something
   through it. It is good that the window should be transparent, because the street or garden beyond it is opaque. How
   if you saw through the garden too? It is no use trying to
   "see through" first principles [of morality]. If you see
   through everything, then everything is transparent, but a
   wholly transparent world is an invisible world. To "see
   through" all things is the same as not to see (p. 91).

6.3 Is faith (trust) wisdom or ignorance?

The Lord of the Rings never shows us a choice for or against
any explicitly religious or supernatural faith. But it shows us
many choices for or against natural faith as a way of knowing.
   It is the Hobbits who best exemplify the epistemological

---

[3] C. S. Lewis, "Meditation in a Toolshed", in *God in the Dock* (Grand
Rapids, Mich.: Eerdmans, 1970), pp. 212–13.

virtue of faith because of their humility. Humility is not only a moral virtue but an epistemological virtue too. The Hobbits show this virtue because they are relatively innocent and childlike (and sometimes even child*ish*, which is *not* a virtue); and this apparent weakness, surprisingly, is their strength—as Gandalf, alone among the great Wizards, sees (LOTR, p. 264). Sauron and Saruman both discount the Hobbits, to their peril. Both have their kingdoms destroyed by the work of the Hobbits!

Jesus makes childlike trust the prerequisite for entering His kingdom: "Unless you turn and become like children, you will never enter the kingdom of heaven" (Mt 18:3). Tolkien says something similar:

> There is a truth in Andrew Lang's words (sentimental though they may sound): "He who would enter into the Kingdom of Faërie should have the heart of a little child." For that possession is necessary to all high adventure, into kingdoms both less and far greater than Faërie. But humility and innocence—these things "the heart of a child" must mean in such a context—do not necessarily imply an uncritical wonder, nor indeed an uncritical tenderness ("On Fairy-Stories", p. 43).

Faith is not foolish or irrational.

C. S. Lewis's essay "On Obstinacy in Belief" is the clearest rational justification I know of faith as a way of reliable knowing that goes beyond reason but yet is perfectly reasonable. It is the answer to those who would criticize Tolkien or his heroes for being naïve and irrational for trusting:

> [T]he scientist thinks it his duty to proportion the strength of his belief exactly to the evidence; to believe less as there is less evidence and to withdraw belief altogether when reliable adverse evidence turns up. . . . [This is called "Clifford's Rule" in philosophy.]

If, for the first time, a doubt of his wife's fidelity crosses the scientist's mind, does he consider it his duty at once to entertain this doubt with complete impartiality, at once to evolve a series of experiments by which it can be tested, and to await the result with pure neutrality of mind? . . .

There are times when we can do all that a fellow creature needs only if he will trust us. In getting a dog out of a trap, in extracting a thorn from a child's finger, in teaching a boy to swim or rescuing one who can't, in getting a frightened beginner over a nasty place on a mountain, the one fatal obstacle may be their distrust. We are asking them . . . to accept apparent impossibilities: that moving the paw farther back into the trap is the way to get it out—that hurting the finger very much more will stop the finger hurting—that water which is obviously permeable will resist and support the body— that holding onto the only support within reach is not the way to avoid sinking—that to go higher and onto a more exposed ledge is the way not to fall. To support all these *incredibilia* we can rely only on the other party's confidence in us—a confidence certainly not based on demonstration. . . .

We are to God, always, as that dog or child or bather or mountain climber was to us, only very much more so. . . . If human life is in fact ordered by a beneficent being whose knowledge of our real needs and of the way in which they can be satisfied infinitely exceeds our own, we must expect *a priori* that His operations will often appear to us far from being beneficent and far from wise. . . .

You are no longer faced with an argument which demands your assent, but with a Person who demands your confidence . . . the assent, of necessity, moves us from the logic of speculative thought into what might perhaps be called the logic of personal relations (*World's Last Night*, pp. 13, 22–24, 26, 29–30).

6.4 What is truth?

"What is truth?" Mortimer Adler says this is one of the easiest questions in philosophy to answer, and he quotes Aristotle's quintessentially commonsensical definition of truth: "When one says of what is that it is, and of what is not that it is not, he speaks the truth."

The most philosophically provocative part of "On Fairy-Stories" is what Tolkien says about fairy stories being "true".

> It is . . . essential to a genuine fairy-story . . . that it should be presented as "true." . . .
> Probably every writer making a secondary world, a fantasy, every sub-creator, wishes in some measure to be a real maker, or hopes that he is drawing on reality: hopes that the peculiar quality of this secondary world (if not all the details) are derived from Reality, or are flowing into it. . . . The peculiar quality of the "joy" in successful Fantasy can thus be explained as a sudden glimpse of the underlying reality or truth. It is not only a "consolation" for the sorrow of this world, but a satisfaction, and an answer to that question, "Is it true?" . . . In the "eucatastrophe" we see in a brief vision that the answer may be greater—it may be a far-off gleam or echo of *evangelium* [gospel, good news] in the real world. . . . All tales may come true; and yet, at the last, redeemed, they may be as like and as unlike the forms that we give them as Man, finally redeemed, will be like and unlike the fallen, that we know ("On Fairy-Stories", pp. 87–90).

Truth is objective, and discovered. Mere fictions are subjective creations. Yet, like many great authors, Tolkien found the process of writing *The Lord of the Rings* to be one of discovery rather than creation. Tolkien's son Christopher said of his father's writing: "I say *discover* because that is how he himself saw it, as he once said, 'Always I had the sense of recording what was already *there*, somewhere; not of *inventing*'" (*Silmarillion*, Foreword, p. 9).

And Tolkien says he wrote *The Lord of the Rings* to elucidate "truth": "I would claim, if I did not think it presumptuous in one so ill-instructed, to have as one object the elucidation of truth, and the encouragement of good morals in this real world, by the ancient device of exemplifying them in unfamiliar embodiments, that may tend to 'bring them home'" (*Letters*, no. 153, p. 194).

But *The Lord of the Rings* is myth, not fact. How can it be "true"? C. S. Lewis explains how a myth can teach a truth more powerfully than anything else can:

> Human intellect is incurably abstract. . . . Yet the only realities we experience are concrete—this pain, this pleasure, this dog, this man. While we are loving the man, bearing the pain, enjoying the pleasure, we are not intellectually apprehending Pleasure, Pain or Personality. When we begin to do so, on the other hand, the concrete realities sink to the level of mere instances or examples. . . . This is our dilemma—either to taste and not to know or to know and not to taste. . . . You cannot *study* Pleasure in the moment of the nuptial embrace, nor repentance while repenting, nor analyse the nature of humour while roaring with laughter. But when else can you really know these things? . . .
>
> Of this tragic dilemma myth is the partial solution. In the enjoyment of a great myth we come nearest to experiencing as a concrete what can otherwise be understood only as an abstraction.[4]

---

[4] C. S. Lewis, "Myth Become Fact", in *God in the Dock*, pp. 65–66.

7

Philosophy of History

7.1 Is history a story?

Probably the most important question in the philosophy of history is whether history is teleological, that is, purposive, providential, plotted, planned, or predestined. Is it a story, with a meaning, or is it "just one damned thing after another"?

To see the difference, contrast two famous poetic expressions of the two opposite answers. One is the Hobbits' humble Walking Song (LOTR, p. 72), which sees life—the life of the individual, of the community, and of the larger community of communities that is the world—as a Road, that "goes ever on and on", that has an objective nature and meaning and direction of its own, and presents to us tasks so that "I must follow if I can", even though we know little and "cannot say" the future.

The opposite philosophy is that history is no story at all. That is Macbeth's philosophy of history:

> Tomorrow, and tomorrow, and tomorrow
> Creeps in this petty pace from day to day
> To the last syllable of recorded time.
> And all our yesterdays have lighted fools
> The way to dusty death. Out! Out, brief candle!
> Life's but a walking shadow, a poor player

That struts and frets his hour upon the stage
And then is heard no more. It is a tale
Told by an idiot, full of sound and fury,
Signifying nothing (*Macbeth*, Act V, scene v)

This is Hell's philosophy of history, for Macbeth is a damned soul, and he is already seeing life as the damned see it.

Once, when our civilization believed in gods (Zeus, Jupiter, JHWH, Jesus), we understood our history to be part of a grand story. We pitied poor damned souls like Macbeth and wrote cautionary tales about them, like Marlowe's *Dr. Faustus*. But our culture has turned inside out, so that it is no longer on the outside of Macbeth, looking in at him with pity and terror, but inside Macbeth's mind, looking out at a world as objectively meaningless as his, full of sound and fury, signifying nothing. And because our culture is thus not "looking at" Macbeth but "looking along" him (to use C. S. Lewis's distinction—see pages 124–25), it is not writing moralistic plays like Shakespeare's, but "naturalistic" novels like Faulkner's *The Sound and the Fury*, showing what life looks like when its teleological frame is removed. Goethe also does this in his great revision of the Faust story by transforming Faust from a damned villain into a clever hero, by transforming the Christian God of moral goodness into the pantheistic God beyond good and evil, and by transforming the devil from God's enemy and Faust's terror into God's own dark side and half of Faust's fulfillment.

Myth and fantasy show us the significance of our lives, and, when done on a large and epic scale, of our history. By *not* showing us particular historical facts that we all know, a fantasy like *The Lord of the Rings* shows us more clearly the grander universal truth that we have forgotten: the truth that these particulars form a meaningful pattern, like threads on the back of the tapestry, deliberately, not randomly, arranged. What greater service could literature perform for us than that? What mythic search is greater than "man's search for meaning"? What issue is more momentous than whether history is "chance or the dance"? [1]

When we see our lives from this higher point of view, we share in a tiny bit of God's mind. That is ultimately why we love literature, according to Tolkien:

> If lit. teaches us anything at all, it is this: that we have in us an eternal element, free from care and fear, which can survey the things that in "life" we call evil with serenity (that is not without appreciating their [evil] quality, but without any disturbance of our spiritual equilibrium). Not in the same way, but in some such way, we shall all doubtless survey our own story when we know it (and a great deal more of the Whole Story) (*Letters*, no. 94, pp. 106–7).

C. S. Lewis points out that the single most important question in morality, in ethics, is really this question in the philosophy of history, the question of the meaning of life:

> Think of us as a fleet of ships sailing in formation. The voyage will be a success only, in the first place, if the ships do not collide and get in one another's way; and, secondly, if each ship is seaworthy and has her engines in good order. . . .
>
> But there is one thing we have not yet taken into account. We have not asked where the fleet is trying to get to. . . . However well the fleet sailed, its voyage would be a failure if it were meant to reach New York and actually arrived in Calcutta.

---

[1] See Victor Frankl, *Man's Search for Meaning* (New York: Pocket Books, 1984); Thomas Howard, *Chance or the Dance?* (San Francisco: Ignatius Press, 1989).

Morality, then, seems to be concerned with three things. Firstly, with fair play and harmony between individuals. Secondly, with what might be called tidying up or harmonizing the things inside each individual. Thirdly, with the general purpose of human life as a whole: what man was made for: what course the whole fleet ought to be on. . . . You may have noticed that modern people are nearly always thinking about the first thing and forgetting the other two (*Mere Christianity*, pp. 70–71).

It is this universal meaning in life and history that gives maximal value to the life of the individual:

If individuals live only seventy years, then a state, or a nation, or a civilization, which may last for a thousand years, is more important than an individual. But if Christianity is true, then the individual is not only more important but incomparably more important, for he is everlasting and the life of a state or a civilization, compared with his, is only a moment (ibid., p. 73).

It is a serious thing to live in a society of possible gods and goddesses, to remember that the dullest and most uninteresting person you can talk to may one day be a creature which, if you saw it now, you would be strongly tempted to worship, or else a horror and a corruption such as you now meet, if at all, only in a nightmare. All day long we are, in some degree, helping each other to one or other of these destinations. It is in the light of these overwhelming possibilities, it is with the awe and circumspection proper to them, that we should conduct all our dealings with one another, all friendships, all loves, all play, all politics. There are no ordinary people. You have never talked to a mere mortal. Nations, cultures, arts, civilisations—these are mortal, and their life is to ours as the life of a gnat. But it is immortals whom we joke with, work with, marry, snub, and exploit—immortal horrors or everlasting splendours.[2]

7.2 Is the past (tradition) a prison or a lighthouse?

Humility entails learning from others. Learning from others entails respect for tradition, for tradition is simply learning from dead others. As Chesterton famously said, tradition is "the democracy of the dead".

The two commonest alternatives in the philosophy of history are traditionalism or radicalism, conservatism or progressivism—to focus primary attention on learning from the past or planning for the future. Tolkien is a conservative. All pre-modern societies were. Perhaps most of the masses in many modern societies still are. Their common sense will not let them believe that it is more important to invent new things than to use and enjoy the ones we already have. Most people are bourgeois, most people are Hobbits, most people are conservatives. But the teachers, the intellectuals, are massively progressives. That is part of the reason for Tolkien's great unpopularity among the critics and his great popularity among their pupils, the masses, who have been deprived of this gospel of the goodness of tradition by their teachers.

There are many meanings to the concept "modern", but common to all of them is the opposition to tradition, the sense that the wisdom of the past has dissipated like a rainbow, the sense that (as Karl Marx put it) "all that is solid melts into air." Tolkien refutes this with a book that makes even its critics marvel at the solidity of Middle-earth and of its history and traditions.

---

[2] C. S. Lewis, *The Weight of Glory and Other Addresses*, rev. ed. (New York: Macmillan, 1980), pp. 18–19.

The basic argument for tradition is simply that it works. It works in *The Lord of the Rings*, over and over again. There are many close calls and dangerous turns in the plot, and most of them would not have been negotiated successfully if the protagonists had not known and followed tradition. They remember something their enemies forget.

It is almost always *words*. Often it is a proverb or riddle or poem. To a culture that scorned tradition, Tolkien offers an epic that exalts *linguistic* traditions, which were not only his professional specialty, but his love.

There are more than five hundred references in *The Lord of the Rings* to the past two ages of Middle-earth. Clyde Kilby counts six hundred in *The Lord of the Rings* and *The Hobbit* together.[3] Tolkien's heroes are humble and therefore look to the past, to the wisdom they had been *given*. His villains and fools are proud and therefore scorn tradition and look only within themselves for their wisdom.

Tolkien is implicitly asking his readers, his culture, to remember their links with their own ancient wisdoms—pagan, Jewish, and Christian. Few lessons, however indirectly taught, could be more socially relevant than this one, for tradition means linking, unifying over time; and no community can exist without common unity over time as well as place. A generation gap destroys a community more surely than a war.

Most people are traditionalists and thus sympathize with a passage like this:

> The notion that motor-cars are more "alive" than, say, centaurs or dragons is curious; that they are more "real" than, say, horses is pathetically absurd. . . .
>
> I do not think that the reader or the maker of fairy-stories need ever be ashamed of the "escape" of

---

[3] Kilby, *Tolkien and the Silmarillion*, p. 45.

archaism. . . . For it is after all possible for a rational man, after reflection, . . . to arrive at the condemnation . . . of progressive things like factories, or the machine-guns and bombs that appear to be their most natural and inevitable, dare we say "inexorable," products ("On Fairy-Stories", pp. 80–82).

C. S. Lewis too was a conservative and called progressivism "the vulgarest of all vulgar errors, that of idolizing as the goddess History what manlier ages belaboured as the strumpet Fortune".[4]

Progressivism is "chronological snobbery", he wrote,

the uncritical acceptance of the intellectual climate common to our own age and the assumption that whatever has gone out of date is on that account discredited. You must find why it went out of date. Was it ever refuted (and if so by whom, where, and how conclusively) or did it merely die away as fashions do? If the latter, this tells us nothing about its truth or falsehood (*Surprised by Joy*, pp. 207–8).

Progressivism is arrogant, for we know the past far better than we know the future: "We have no notion what stage in the journey we have reached. Are we in Act I or Act V? Are our present diseases those of childhood or senility? . . . A story is precisely the sort of thing that cannot be understood until you have heard the whole of it" (*Christian Reflections*, p. 106).

Tolkien's traditionalism, with all its dependence on the past, does not make the mistake of ignoring the future. In fact, the main reason for tradition is to guide the future. It is not even accurate to say that Tolkien's heroes *balance* their traditionalism with a sense of responsibility for the future, as

[4] C. S. Lewis, "Historicism", in *Christian Reflections* (Grand Rapids, Mich.: Eerdmans, 1967), p. 102.

if the two things were opposites. For listening to the past and responsibility for the future are two sides of the same coin.

7.3 Is history predictable?

Tolkien is not a progressivist, but he does not embrace the opposite error either, the notion that "there is nothing new under the sun", that history is a set of unending and unchangeable cycles of doom. That was the standard pagan philosophy of history as fate. Tolkien's Christian philosophy of history avoids both the false pessimism of pre-Christian paganism and the false optimism of post-Christian humanism.

Tolkien mentions the importance of individual acts as one of *The Lord of the Rings'* major themes:

> the place in "world politics" of the unforeseen and unforeseeable acts of will, and deeds of virtue of the apparently small, ungreat, forgotten in the places of the Wise and Great (good as well as evil). A moral of the whole . . . is the obvious one that without the high and noble the simple and vulgar is utterly mean; and without the simple and ordinary the noble and heroic is meaningless (*Letters*, no. 131, p. 160).

In the Christian philosophy of history there are things that are genuinely new because there is a God above time who can alter history. God says, "Behold, I am doing a new thing" (Is 43:19). History does not simply repeat itself, and the future cannot be predicted. Paganism tried to understand history in terms of the cycles of nature, but the Bible understands nature in terms of history, as the setting for the drama between man and God and between man and man.

Tom Bombadil shows the relation between nature and history in Tolkien. Tom seems to be a personification of nature, or a nature spirit. He is probably Aulë, the angel of the earth. In contrast,

The Ring itself is a historical being. It is a product of historical purpose and action and its meaning is a historical meaning. . . .
In some way he [Bombadil] represents nature, and Tolkien uses him to identify the essentially historical by contrast. Tom asked about the Ring, but did not seem to take it very seriously; moreover, it had no power over him. It did not make him invisible, and, when Frodo put it on, Tom could still see him. The affair of the Ring was history, and Tom's was not a historical existence. At the Council of Elrond one of the elves suggested that they ask Tom Bombadil to take the Ring and hide it in the Old Forest. Gandalf answered that, if Tom could be persuaded to, he would not understand the need and would soon forget it or even more likely throw it away. "Such things have no hold on his mind." . . . Glorfindel said, "I think that in the end, if all else is conquered, Bombadil will fall, Last as he was First; and then Night will come" (I, 279). Glorfindel, it should be noted, did not *predict* such an outcome; the Council did not despair. But historical decision is ultimately what determines nature and not the other way round. In Tolkien's "monotheistic world," the mysterious Authority which is in control of history is One for whom nature itself is a historical act.[5]

The theological basis for this is the difference between Men and angels:

[5] Willis Glover, "The Christian Character of Tolkien's Invented World", in *Criticism: A Quarterly Journal for Literature and the Arts*, vol. 13, no. 1 (Winter 1971), pp. 48–49.

The dealings of the Ainur have indeed been mostly with the Elves, for Iluvatar made them more like in nature to the Ainur, though less in might and stature, whereas to Men he gave strange gifts. . . . He willed that the hearts of Men should seek beyond the world and should find no rest therein; but they should have a virtue to shape their life, amid the powers and chances of the world, beyond the music of the Ainur, which is as fate to all things else. . . . It is one with this gift of freedom that the children of Men dwell only a short space in the world alive, and are not bound to it, and depart soon (*The Silmarillion*, pp. 41–42).

Note the connection between (1) the freedom in man's life and history, (2) his materiality and temporality, (3) his mortality, and (4) his restless longing (*Sehnsucht*). Angels are (1) transcendent to history, (2) immaterial, (3) immortal, and (4) complete.

Paradoxically, our freedom is our doom: we are doomed not only to restlessness and to death but also to freedom. Our free-*dom* is a free *doom*:

"What doom do you bring out of the North?"
"The doom of choice," said Aragorn (LOTR, p. 423).

C. S. Lewis writes about the unpredictability of history too:

About everything that can be called "the philosophy of history" I am a desperate sceptic. I know nothing of the future, not even whether there will be any future. . . . I don't know whether the human tragi-comedy is now in Act I or Act V, whether our present disorders are those of infancy or old age. [6]

[6] This 1955 essay, "*De Descriptione Temporum*", was Lewis's Cambridge University inaugural lecture as Professor of Medieval and Renaissance English Literature. Reprinted in *Selected Literary Essays*, ed. Walter Hooper (Cambridge, Eng.: Cambridge University Press, 1969), p. 3; also in C. S. Lewis, *They Asked for a Paper: Papers and Addresses* (London: Geoffrey Bles, 1962), p. 12.

7.4 Is there devolution as well as evolution?

Throughout *The Lord of the Rings*, most great things, great deeds, great heroes, and great ages are in the past.

Clearly Tolkien believed that his century, the twentieth, was spiritually smaller, in its virtues and even in its vices, than medieval Christendom; less heroic than the "Dark Ages" that produced *Beowulf;* and uglier than the Victorian and Edwardian eras, which Tolkien saw passing away before his eyes. *The Lord of the Rings* can be viewed as a mythical history of how tawdry modern ages like our own come to be.

Devolution is the consequence of violating the Principle of First and Second Things (see pages 150–51). When beauty is sacrificed for efficiency, the result is inefficiency. When men worship machines, the proper good not only of man but also of machines is sacrificed.

Consider the evidence. In the past, there were few machines and many slaves; and the rich, who could afford many slaves, lived a life of leisure because of them. Today, when machines have replaced slaves (an obvious advance), those rich enough to afford the most machines do *not* have more leisure than they had before, but less!

Leisure means time, or control over your time, i.e., liberty. Machines were supposed to give liberty both to the slaves, who were no longer needed, and to the masters, by maximizing their leisure. Every technological power is a power over time, a way of saving time, whether for traveling (fast cars), cooking (microwave ovens), or communicating (computers). Yet everyone complains about having *less* leisure, less "free time" than ever before. Our parents had more time for us than we have for our children; and their parents had more time for them than they had for us. Most of us *spend* more time paying for, learning, relearning, cursing, servicing, up-dating, and playing with our computers than we *save* with them.

But there is hope. After Sauron's defeat Aragorn ushers in a new golden age. Yet this is only temporary. *Every* victory over evil is. Aragorn's descendants gradually lose his nobility, and the pattern repeats.

The pattern is free, yet it is cyclic: (1) divine blessings, (2) consequent human prosperity, (3) the fall into pride and laziness, (4) consequent decline, (5) disaster, which stirs (6) repentance, which brings as its result (1) divine blessings again. This is the repeated pattern of the history of Israel in the Bible, and it is the universal pattern for the history of all nations. For Israel, like Christ, is the rule as well as the exception, the key to universal history as well as the unique center of it.

Whether one's personal temperament is optimistic or pessimistic, any realistic philosophy of history must account for decline. Universal optimism and the idea of universal necessary progress are simply silly. As C. S. Lewis puts it, "It is, indeed, manifestly not the case that there is any law of progress in ethical, cultural, and social history" (*World's Last Night*, pp. 103–4).

See also the interaction between Merlin, who is resuscitated to help modern England in her spiritually darkest hour, as some had hoped King Arthur would do with the twentieth century, in Lewis's *That Hideous Strength* (pp. 292–93).

7.5 Is human life a tragedy or a comedy?

A pessimist like Tolkien can be a happy man. Both Tolkien and Lewis, who were traditionalists, conservatives, and pessimists rather than progressives, had an optimistic attitude toward ordinary life. Both lived good lives even in a purely material sense: they were able to enjoy the simple, best things in life, such as walking and weather and conversation with friends. We find the opposite connection on the part of the ideological Left, between their desperately optimistic philosophy of history and their inability to admit or enjoy ordinary, earthy Hobbit-like bourgeois pleasures. Indeed, no word is more despicable in the Marxist vocabulary than "bourgeois".

Tolkien was not an optimist by temperament but by conviction. Had he philosophized by feeling rather than faith, he would never have been able to make both halves of this statement, in 1944:

> I sometimes feel appalled at the thought of the sum total of human misery. . . . If anguish were visible, almost the whole of this benighted planet would be enveloped in a dense dark vapour. . . . But . . . evil labours with vast power and perpetual success—in vain: preparing always only the soil for unexpected good to sprout in (*Letters*, no. 64, p. 76).

Tolkien knows this by faith in the God who joins goodness and power in one being. But he also knows it by philosophical reason, for evil is a parasite on good; being as such is good. Therefore the more evil a thing is, the more it approaches nonbeing. Evil is self-destructive.

Whether or not "optimism" is the right word for Tolkien's temperament, it is the wrong word for his philosophy. The right one is "hope". The chances of history coming out well seem slim. But it happens. And it is precisely because the chances of salvation seem so slim that the victory is very precious—as Tolkien explains in "On Fairy-Stories".

The Eucatastrophe, or Happy Ending, is not only consolation but truth—if the gospel, the "good news", is not a lie.

From the premise that Christianity is true it follows that the far-off glimpse of joy produced by fantasy is a glimpse of truth; that a great eucatastrophic tale like *The Lord of the Rings* is a gift of divine grace, an opening of the curtain that veils Heaven to earthly eyes, a tiny telepathic contact with the Mind of God.

There are at least two great eucatastrophes in *The Lord of the Rings*. The most dramatic one is at the Crack of Doom. Sam and Frodo are at the end of their road, utterly hopeless and prepared to die. One of Frodo's fingers has already fallen into the Crack of Doom, surrounded by the Ring and Gollum's teeth; and the rest of Frodo and Sam are about to follow when Mount Orodruin erupts. But Frodo has completed his Quest: this is his joy. As for Sam, Frodo's return from what could be called spiritual death is *his* joy. Sam sees Frodo "pale and worn, and yet himself again. . . . 'Master!' cried Sam, and fell upon his knees. In all that ruin of the world, for the moment he felt only joy, great joy. The burden was gone. His master had been saved; he was himself again, he was free" (LOTR, p. 926).

It is not his physical survival afterward that is the eucatastrophe. Had he died, as most epic heroes do (e.g., Arthur and Beowulf), the eucatastrophe would have been unmarred— just as Job would have been happy in the end even if he had *not* recovered his health, possessions, and family, so long as he saw God. The essential triumph is spiritual.

The joy of both Frodo and Sam is pure and poignant because of their unselfish love: Sam for Frodo, Frodo for the Shire and all of Middle-earth, which he has saved. They are not "winners". They are wounded and ready to die, and they have succeeded only by an incredible grace, not by force of mind or body, plans or arms. Frodo, in fact, failed; it was Gollum who completed the impossible task. The nearly miraculous outcome leaves the reader no room for pride or self-righteousness, as many "happy endings" do.

The second eucatastrophe is described more honorifically—in fact, liturgically. It resembles what we will surely experience in Heaven. This comes just a little later, after the rescue. Here too it is Frodo's honor that is the source of Sam's joy:

Gandalf stood before him robed in white. . . . "Well, Master Samwise, how do you feel?" he said.

But Sam lay back and stared with open mouth, and for a moment, between bewilderment and great joy, he could not answer. At last he gasped: "Gandalf! I thought you were dead! But then I thought I was dead myself. Is everything sad going to come untrue? What's happened to the world?"

"A great Shadow has departed," said Gandalf, and then he laughed, and the sound was like music, or like water in a parched land; and as he listened the thought came to Sam that he had not heard laughter, the pure sound of merriment, for days upon days without count. It fell on his ears like the echo of all the joys he had ever known. And he burst into tears. . . .

And then, to Sam's final and complete satisfaction and pure joy, a minstrel of Gondor stood forth, and knelt, and begged leave to sing. And behold! He said: ". . . I will sing to you of Frodo of the Nine Fingers and the Ring of Doom."

And when Sam heard that, he laughed aloud for sheer delight, and he stood up and cried, "O great glory and splendour! And all my wishes have come true!" And then he wept.

And all the host laughed and wept, and in the midst of their merriment and tears the clear voice of the minstrel rose like silver and gold, and all men were hushed. And he sang to them, now in the Elven-tongue, now in the speech of the West, until their hearts, wounded with sweet words, overflowed, and their joy was like swords, and they passed in thought out to regions where pain and delight flow together and tears are the very wine of blessedness (LOTR, pp. 930–931, 933).

We are that laughing and weeping host, and Tolkien is our minstrel.

Eucatastrophe, of course, is almost the opposite of "progressivism". Both are "happy endings", but the first is sheer grace, while the second is necessity. We are "surprised by joy" in eucatastrophe, while we are surprised by evil and failure if we are "progressives".

The *locus classicus* in Lewis for the refutation of progressivism is "The Funeral of a Great Myth". The myth he refutes in this essay is not just historical optimism but also the more general cosmic progressivism, evolutionism, or optimism that it exemplifies. After praising this cosmic Myth of Progress for its imaginative power (man, the unlikely hero, evolving from slime, outlasting dinosaurs, becoming cleverer and cleverer— "Let no one say we are an unimaginative age: neither the Greeks nor the Norsemen ever invented a better story"), he gives its logical refutation, noting

> the fatal self-contradiction which runs right through it. . . . The Myth asks me to believe that reason is simply the unforeseen and unintended by-product of a mindless process at one stage of its endless and aimless becoming. The content of the Myth thus knocks from under me the only ground on which I could possibly believe the Myth to be true. If my own mind is a product of the irrational— if what seem my clearest reasonings are only the way in which a creature conditioned as I am is bound to feel—how shall I trust my mind when it tells me about

Evolution? . . . The fact that some people of scientific education cannot by any effort be taught to see the difficulty, confirms one's suspicion that we here touch a radical disease in their whole style of thought.[7]

What accounts for this blind spot? Lewis goes on to explain:

The basic idea of the Myth—that small or chaotic or feeble things perpetually turn themselves into large, strong, ordered things—may, at first sight, seem a very odd one. We have never actually seen a pile of rubble turning itself into a house. But this odd idea commends itself to the imagination by the help of what seem to be two instances of it within everyone's knowledge. Everyone has seen individual organisms doing it. Acorns become oaks, grubs become insects, eggs become birds, every man was once an embryo. And secondly—which weighs very much in the popular mind during a machine age—everyone has seen Evolution really happening in the history of machines. We all remember when locomotives were smaller and less efficient than they are now. These two apparent instances are quite enough to convince the imagination that Evolution in a cosmic sense is the most natural thing in the world. [But] . . . reason cannot here agree with imagination. These apparent instances are not really instances of Evolution at all. The oak comes indeed from the acorn, but then the acorn was dropped by an earlier oak. Every man begins with the union of an ovum and a spermatozoon, but the ovum and the spermatozoon came from two fully developed human beings. The modern express engine came from the *Rocket*: but the *Rocket* came, not from something more elementary than itself but from something much more developed and highly organized—the mind of a man, and a man of genius (ibid., p. 90).

---

[7] Lewis, "The Funeral of a Great Myth", in *Christian Reflections*, pp. 88–89.

Aesthetics

Of all the divisions of philosophy, this one seems the most resistant to analysis. What is beauty, and why does it move us so? Only a few threads are clear in this rope that tugs on our hearts. One of them is glory.

8.1 Why do we no longer love glory or splendor?

Glory and splendor are certainly neither modern nor "familiar". Yet they contribute not only to beauty but also to joy, to human fulfillment. If we are created for royal glory, then royal glory will fulfill us, however unfashionable our ideology makes it.

The things in *The Lord of the Rings* that reflect this glory are manifold, and include humble, Hobbit-like things as well as exalted, Elvish things. Words and language reveal them, and it is not clear whether it is the glory of the things that justifies the words or the glory of the words that justifies the things. The original inspiration for *The Lord of the Rings* was linguistic. "In the beginning was the Word" for Tolkien as for God.

C. S. Lewis saw *The Lord of the Rings* as a near miracle largely because of its high style and its effect on the human spirit. His review of volume one began thus: "This book is lightning from a clear sky. . . . The names alone are a feast. . . . They embody that piercing, high, Elvish beauty of

8

68

which no other prose writer has captured so much. . . . Here
are beauties which pierce like swords or burn like cold iron;
here is a book that will break your heart." [1]

In fact, Lewis's aesthetic centers on just this: the power to
break hearts.

> Have you not seen that in our days
> Of any whose story, song, or art
> Delights us, our sincerest praise
> Means, when all's said, 'You break my heart'? [2]

In *An Experiment in Criticism* Lewis defines a great book as
one that elicits great reading, and he defines great reading as
conjuring up great literary experiences, such as wonder and
joy—exactly why Tolkien said he wrote *The Lord of the Rings*;
in his foreword to the second edition he wrote, "The prime
motive was the desire of a tale-teller to try his hand at a really
long story that would hold the attention of readers, amuse
them, delight them, and at times maybe excite them or
deeply move them" (LOTR, p. xvi).

Lewis explains the high style of epic in *A Preface to "Paradise Lost"*. Though he is speaking of poetry, especially
Milton's, what he says is also true of epic prose like Tolkien's,
especially in *The Silmarillion*. Epic has

> a quality. . . which moderns find difficult to under-
> stand. . . . The quality will be understood by any one who
> really understands the meaning of the Middle English
> word *solempne*. This means something different, but not
> quite different, from modern English *solemn*. Like *solemn* it
> implies the opposite of what is familiar, free and easy, or
> ordinary. But unlike *solemn* it does not suggest gloom,

---

[1] C. S. Lewis, in *Time and Tide* (August 1954), p. 1082. Reprinted in *C. S.
Lewis: Essay Collection*.

[2] C. S. Lewis, *Poems* (New York: Harcourt Brace, 1992), p. 133.

oppression, or austerity. . . . A great mass by Mozart or Beethoven is as much a solemnity in its hilarious *Gloria* as in its poignant *crucifixus est.* Feasts are, in this sense, *more* solemn than fasts. . . . The very fact that *pompous* is now used only in a bad sense measures the degree to which we have lost the old idea of "solemnity." . . . In an age when every one puts on his oldest clothes to be happy in, you must re-awake the simpler state of mind in which people put on gold and scarlet to be happy in. Above all, you must be rid of the hideous idea, fruit of a widespread inferiority complex, that pomp, on the proper occasions, has any connexion with vanity or self-conceit. A celebrant approaching the altar, a princess led out by a king to dance a minuet, a general officer on a ceremonial parade, a major-domo preceding the boar's head at a Christmas feast—all these wear unusual clothes and move with calculated dignity. This does not mean that they are vain, but that they are obedient. . . . The modern habit of doing ceremonial things unceremoniously is no proof of humility; rather it proves the offender's inability to forget himself in the rite. . . . We moderns may like dances which are hardly distinguishable from walking and poetry which sounds as if it might be uttered *ex tempore.* Our ancestors did not. They liked a dance which *was* a dance, and fine clothes which no one could mistake for working clothes, and feasts that no one could mistake for ordinary dinners, and poetry that unblushingly proclaimed itself to be poetry. What is the point of having a poet, inspired by the Muse, if he tells the stories just as you or I would have told them? . . . When we are caught up into the experience which a "grand" style communicates, we are, in a sense, no longer conscious of the style. Incense is consumed by being used.[3]

[3] C. S. Lewis, *A Preface to "Paradise Lost"* (New York: Oxford University Press, 1961), pp. 17, 21.

8.2 Is beauty always good?

In Greek there is a word (*kalon*) that means both "good" and "beautiful". This is specified by another word, *k'agathon*, which is a contraction of *to kalon kai to agathon*, "the good-and-beautiful". A great marriage! But in modern times, the two are divorced: moral goodness becomes drab and beauty morally dangerous. Spenser could still woo readers of his age by imaging Virtue as a beautiful woman; but a century later Milton could not make people of our age love his God more than his Satan. Aeschylus won civic honors (free room and board in the Town Hall for life) with his religious dramas, but a modern poet is expected to be a social rebel, live in poverty, go insane, and cut off his ear and send it to his mistress.

Tolkien bewailed both the ugliness of his age and its separation between the good and the beautiful. (See "On Fairy-Stories", p. 83.)

But Beauty's moral danger seems to be not just in modern culture but in the very nature of things. At all times and places the beauty of a Helen or a Cleopatra has lured men to destruction. A beautiful face often masks an ugly soul. And there have always been beautiful but wicked queens, like the White Witch in Narnia or the Snow Queen in Hans Christian Andersen. And also the reverse: someone like Strider, who seems foul yet feels fair, or like the prophets; the hick town of Nazareth; the cold, dirty stable in Bethlehem; and Calvary—why does God send His best gifts in such ugly wrappings?

The contrast between the good and the beautiful is *not* in the nature of things. Only in a fallen world is beauty a temptation, or "vain" (see Prov 31:30); and that is only because God trains us by what Lewis calls the Principle of "First and

Second Things" in the essay by that title (in *God in the Dock*, pp. 278–81). Putting first things first is the key to the health of second things. Beauty is a "second thing": it is very good, but not as good as moral goodness. And the worship of "art for art's sake" will destroy not only true worship but also art. An example of this Principle of "First and Second Things" in *The Silmarillion* is Feanor, who puts his own greatest work of art, the Silmarils, before his moral duty. He will not give up the jewels, just as in *The Lord of the Rings* the proud will not give up the Ring. Feanor envies the Valar and refuses his duty and his destiny—unlike Frodo. Even Niggle (Tolkien's gently self-mocking self-portrait in "Leaf by Niggle") had to learn the principle that art must be put second to morality, his painting second to his needy neighbor (Parish).

But this way of putting it is misleading, as if beauty and goodness were separate entities that could in principle clash. Rather, beauty is one of the more important forms *of* goodness: beauty is very *good*. And goodness is the highest form of beauty: the most beautiful thing in this world is a saint. Both goodness and beauty are eternal and essential attributes of Ultimate Reality, the One God, and therefore are ultimately one.

Beauty is the bloom on the rose of goodness and truth, the child conceived by their union; and thus it is not only good but Heavenly. And while beauty cannot of itself save us or substitute for either goodness or truth (contrary to Keats's moving but muddled sentiment that "beauty is truth, truth beauty; that is all you know on earth and all you need to know"), yet it contributes toward the salvation of the creation. For it is the opposite of reductionism. In Heaven the poets "shall have flames upon their heads".

We humans need beauty as well as morality in our lives. And the reason is that we are made in God's image, and God is the most creative of artists. Tolkien calls us subcreators and notes that "we make still by the law in which we're made" ("On Fairy-Stories", p. 74).

The Principle of "First and Second Things" applies to the relation between beauty and efficiency (a "Third Thing") as well as beauty and moral goodness (a "First Thing"). Just as you lose beauty if you sacrifice morality for it, so you lose efficiency if you sacrifice beauty for it—as Tom Shippey sagely points out, commenting on "The Scouring of the Shire":

> "This country wants waking up and setting to rights," says the leader of the Hobbiton ruffians, as though he had some goal beyond mere hatred and contempt for the Shire, and . . . it seems to be more industrialization, efficiency, economy of effort, all things often and still wished on the population of Britain. The trouble with that (as developments after the publication of *The Lord of the Rings* have tended to confirm), was that the products of efficiency-drives were often not only soulless but also inefficient. Why do Sharkey's men knock down perfectly satisfactory old houses and put up in their place damp, ugly, badly-built, standardized ones? No one ever explains, but the overall picture was one all too familiar to post-war Britons. . . . The Sarumans of the world rule by deluding their followers with images of a technological Paradise. . . . But what one often gets (as has become only more obvious since Tolkien's time) are the blasted landscapes of Eastern Europe, strip-mined and polluted, and even radioactive.[4]

Beauty can also be goodness's prophet (LOTR, p. 901).

[4] Shippey, *J. R. R. Tolkien*, pp. 168, 171.

9

Philosophy of Language

The goal of philosophy is "Logos". Logos, like its Chinese counterpart "Tao", is an incomparably profound and multivalent word that means essentially three things: (1) the ultimate nature of things, the one source of all essential reality and intelligibility; (2) intelligence, understanding, wisdom, truth, as *the knowledge of* that essential reality; and (3) communication, language, speech, argument, explanation, or word, *the expression of* that knowledge. Philosophy studies all three: the first is metaphysics, the second is epistemology, and the third is philosophy of language. Pre-modern philosophy specialized in the first, classical modern philosophy in the second, and post-modern philosophy in the third.

9.1 How can words be alive?

Words were to Tolkien the most beautiful things in the world. That would be a ridiculous preference for a Hindu or Buddhist, but not for a Christian, for whom the most beautiful thing human eyes have ever seen is called "the Word of God".

Tolkien loved words (especially proper names) so much that he gave all his favorite things many names, not just one, and lingered long and lovingly over the art of naming:

Taniquetil the Elves name that holy mountain, and
Oiolossë Everlasting Whiteness, and Elerrina Crowned
with Stars, and many names beside; but the Sindar spoke
of it in their later tongue as Amon Uilos. . . . Telperion
the one was called in Valinor, and Silpio, and Ninquelótë,
and many other names; but Laurelin the other was, and
Malinalda, and Culúrien, and many names in song beside
(*Silmarillion*, pp. 37–38).

It is as T. S. Eliot says, in his sage advice at the beginning of
"Old Possum's Book of Practical Cats":

The Naming of Cats is a difficult matter,
It isn't just one of your holiday games;
You may think at first I'm as mad as a hatter
When I tell you, a cat must have THREE
DIFFERENT NAMES.

Words were important to Tolkien, not just instrumentally,
through their power and effect on life, but metaphysically,
through their source and basis and foundation. For "in the
beginning was the Word" (Jn 1:1). A Word—the Word of
God—was the origin of the world (Gen 1:3). And a word
was the origin of *The Hobbit*, and thus its sequel *The Lord of
the Rings*:

All I remember about the start of *The Hobbit* is sitting
correcting School Certificate papers in the everlasting
weariness of that annual task forced on impecunious aca-
demics with children. On a blank leaf I scrawled: "In a
hole in the ground there lived a hobbit." I did not and do
not know why. . . . I did nothing about it, for a long
time. . . . But it became *The Hobbit* in the early 1930s. . . .
Since *The Hobbit* was a success, a sequel was called for
(*Letters*, no. 163, p. 215).

Earlier, Tolkien's whole mythology of *The Silmarillion* and its offspring *The Lord of the Rings* began with words. Tolkien first invented the Elvish language. Then he needed a race to speak it: Elves. Then they needed a history. It was the language that suggested the world and its history to Tolkien, not vice versa.

The same is true of Ents as of Hobbits and Elves: "As usually with me they grew rather out of their name, than the other way about" (*Letters*, no. 157, p. 208).

Tolkien discovered that " 'legends' depend on the language to which they belong. . . . Greek mythology depends far more on the marvelous aesthetic of its language and so of its nomenclature of persons and places and less on its content than people realize" (*Letters*, no. 180, p. 231).

Many readers dislike the plethora of names in *The Lord of the Rings* and, even more, in *The Silmarillion*. One reviewer complained that *The Silmarillion* sounded like "a Swedish railway conductor with a head cold announcing stations". (I would call that a fascinating aural experience!)

The words of much of *The Lord of the Rings* and all of *The Silmarillion* are vertical, and heavy, as Max Picard says of Hebrew:

> The architecture of the language was vertical. Each word sank down vertically, column-wise, into the sentence. In language today we have lost the static quality of the ancient tongues. The sentence has become dynamic; every word and every sentence speeds on to the next . . . each word comes more from the preceding word than from the silence and moves on more to the next word in front than to the silence. . . .
>
> A quiver full of steel arrows, a firmly secured anchor rope, a brazen trumpet splitting the air with its few piercing tones: that is the Hebrew language—it can say little,

but what it says is like the beating of hammers on the anvil.[1]

Each word in *The Silmarillion* seems like a thunderbolt from Heaven, a miracle. There are many capital letters, in contrast with the fashion of our leveling, reductionistic age to trim, to decapitalize, to decapitate. And there are many nouns, both common and proper. It is the Anglo-Saxon style. The words are solid, like mountains; heavy and slow, like a glacier. The sense of height and weight of words suggests the sense of ontological height and weight, a verticality, a supernaturalism. The reader is lifted up out of himself into immense polar skies, into the realm where "great syllables of words that sounded like castles came out of his mouth" (*That Hideous Strength*, p. 228).

9.2 The metaphysics of words: Can words have real power?

But there is more: strange as it sounds, things are *in* words for Tolkien. The language of *The Lord of the Rings*, and even more of *The Silmarillion*, is not merely a device for communicating thoughts and feelings. The words are not mere labels for concepts. Rather, it is *in* the words that the things live and move and have their being; and *in* the words they come to us. As Martin Heidegger puts it, language is "the House of Being". "For words and language are not wrappings in which things are packed for the commerce of those who write and speak. It is in words and language that things first come into being and are. For this reason the misuse of language, in idle talk, in slogans and phrases, destroys our authentic relation to things." [2]

[1] Max Picard, *The World of Silence* (Chicago: Regnery, 1952), pp. 44–45.

[2] Martin Heidegger, *An Introduction to Metaphysics* (New York: Doubleday Anchor, 1961), p. 11.

"This naming does not consist merely in something already known being supplied with a name; it is rather that when the poet speaks the essential word, the existent is by this name nominated as what it is. So it becomes known as existent [real]. Poetry is the establishing of being by means of the word." [3]

Thus poetry is making, as its name says (*poiesis*). Poetry is not ornament but fundamental speech; prose is fallen poetry. And fundamental speech is an act of creating. And unspeaking is uncreating. "Last of all is set the name of Melkor, He Who Arises in Might. But that name he has forfeited, and the Noldor, who among the Elves suffered most from his malice, will not utter it" (*Silmarillion*, p. 31). And Gandalf will not utter the words on the Ring in the language of Mordor in the Shire, but only at the Council of Elrond in Rivendell, and even in that safe and holy place the words summon something of the presence of their Hellish source:

"*Ash nazg durbatuluk, ash nazg gimbatul, ash nazg thrakatuluk agh burzum-ishi krimpatul.*"

The change in the wizard's voice was astounding. Suddenly it became menacing, powerful, harsh as stone. A shadow seemed to pass over the high sun, and the porch for a moment drew dark. All trembled, and the Elves stopped their ears.

"Never before has any voice dared to utter words of that tongue in Imladris, Gandalf the Grey," said Elrond, as the shadow passed and the company breathed once more (LOTR, pp. 247–48).

The power of words is based on the fact that real things are found in words. Words are not merely things among a world of things, things with one additional feature, the ability to

[3] Martin Heidegger, "Holderlin and the Essence of Poetry", in *Existence and Being* (Chicago: Regnery, 1949), p. 304.

point to other things. No, words are the encompassing frame of the world of things. Things constitute a "world" only by the creative word of the author, who names them.

And therefore, since the things are encompassed by words, our wonder at the things is encompassed by our wonder at the words.

The genealogies are the dullest part of the Bible for modern readers, but they were some of the most wonderful for the ancients.

There is a numinous, electrifying scene in the play *Equus* where a boy who has invented a religion of worshipping horses (since there is nothing in his modern world to worship) invokes the many names of his horse-god.

At the end of the movie *Roots*, when the family of slaves finally enters its freedom and its promised land, it solemnizes the event by reciting the account of its origins, the words that had been faithfully handed down for generations: "One day Kunta Kinte went out to fell a tree to make a drum." And then followed the list of ancestral names.

9.3 Are there right and wrong words?

If things come to us in their names, if language is the "house of being", then the power of things comes to us in the power of their names. Words have power, not only to communicate, intellectually, and not only to suggest, emotionally, but also a magical power that can produce physical effects.

There are many examples of this in *The Lord of the Rings*: Bombadil is the clearest one. His words save Merry from Old Man Willow and Frodo from the Barrow-wight, for "*None has ever caught him yet, for Tom, he is the master: His songs are stronger songs, and his feet are faster*" (LOTR, p. 139).

Frodo too uses the "magical" power of words: when he calls Tom's name, two miracles happen, one spiritual and one physical. The name conjures up both Frodo's courage and Tom, who actually comes. If we find this unconvincing, it shows how little we have taken God at His word when He repeatedly promises the same thing Bombadil did. To put the promise in contemporary words, "You just call out My Name, and you know, wherever I am, I'll come running to see you again. . . ."

We know there are words that sacramentally effect what they signify, there are operative words, there are magic words. Two of the most familiar "magic words" are "I love you" and "I hate you." These are not labels for communication; they are spiritual weapons, arrows that pierce through flesh and into hearts. The whole of *The Lord of the Rings* is an armor-piercing rocket that can get even into our underground bunkers.

The most powerful words are proper names, names of persons or places. When the Black Rider bangs on Fatty Bulger's door in Buckland saying, "Open in the name of Mordor", all the authority and power and terror of Mordor are really present there. When Frodo, on Weathertop, faces the Black Rider, "he heard himself crying aloud, '*O Elbereth! Gilthoniel!*'" (LOTR, p. 191), as he struck the Rider with his sword. Afterward, Aragorn says, "All blades perish that pierce that dreadful King. More deadly to him was the name of Elbereth" (LOTR, p. 193).

In Shelob's lair Frodo speaks in tongues again: "'Aiya Earendil Elenion Ancalima!' he cried, and knew not what he had spoken; for it seemed that another voice spoke through his" (LOTR, p. 704). And when the tiny Hobbit with the tiny sword advanced on the most hideous creature in Middle-earth with the phial of Galadriel *and the name of Galadriel*, Shelob cowered.

What's in a name? In the name of Jesus, devils were exorcised, Hell defeated, and Heaven's gates opened for us.
What's in a name? Everything. In a name the whole universe was created.
That name was the Word of God, the Mind of God, the Logos.
What's in a name? Moses asked God that question at the burning bush, and God answered, "I AM."

9.4 Is there an original, universal, natural language?

There is an old myth of an original language. It is in Plato (the "Cratylus") and the Bible (the story of the Tower of Babel, answered by Pentecost). If this is true, it explains why every proper name of Tolkien's seems exactly right. (This is a power even many of his critics marvel at.) When we read them we are *remembering* (Plato's *anamnesis*); our cognition is a recognition. Our "word detector" buzzes when we meet the Right Word, the Platonic Idea, the Jungian Archetype. We experience discovery rather than invention, as when Mercury descends to earth in the "Descent of the Gods" chapter in C. S. Lewis's *That Hideous Strength:*

> It was as if the words spoke themselves through him from some strong place at a distance—or as if they were not words at all but the present operations of God. . . . For this was the language spoken before the Fall and beyond the Moon and the meanings were not given to the syllables by chance, or skill, or long tradition, but truly inherent in them as the shape of the great Sun is inherent in the little water-drop. This was Language herself, as she first sprang at Maleldil's bidding out of the molten quicksilver of the star called Mercury on Earth, but Viritrilbia in Deep Heaven (p. 319).

The most important proper name to you is your own. In C. S. Lewis's anthology of 365 selections from George Mac-Donald, the one most readers find unforgettable is his commentary on Revelation 2:17 ("I will give him a white stone, with a new name written on the stone, which no one knows except him who receives it"):

The giving of the white stone with the new name is the communication of what God thinks about the man to the man. It is the divine judgment, the solemn holy doom of the righteous man, the "Come, thou blessed," spoken to the individual. . . . The true name is one which expresses the character, the nature, the meaning of the person who bears it. It is the man's own symbol—his soul's picture, in a word—the sign which belongs to him and to no one else. Who can give a man this, his own name? God alone. For no one but God sees who the man is. . . . It is only when the man has become his name that God gives him the stone with the name upon it, for then first can he understand what his name signifies. . . . God's name for a man must be the expression of His own idea of the man, that being whom He had in His thought when He began to make the child, and whom He kept in His thought through the long process of creation that went to realize the idea. To tell the name is to seal the success—to say "In thee also I am well pleased." [4]

9.5   Why is music so powerful?

The most powerful and magical language is music. The reason for this is that music is the original language. Music is the language of creation. In *The Silmarillion* (as in Lewis's creation story in *The Magician's Nephew*), God and His angels

[4] C. S. Lewis, *George MacDonald: An Anthology*, pp. 7–8.

sing the world into being:"In the beginning, Eru, the One, who in the Elvish tongue is named Iluvatar, made the Ainur of his thought; and they made a great Music before him. In this Music the World was begun" (*Silmarillion*, p. 25).

It is not that the music was in the world but that the world was in the music. This is "the music of the spheres", *in* which everything is, the "Song of Songs" that includes all songs. All matter, space, time, and history are in this primal language.

Plato knew the power of music. In the *Republic* it is the first step in education in the good society and the first step in corruption in the bad one. Nothing is more powerful to the good society, to education, to human happiness in this world.

Music is not ornamented poetry, and poetry is not ornamented prose. Poetry is fallen music, and prose is fallen poetry. Prose is not the original language; it is poetry made practical. Even poetry is not the original language; it is music made speakable, it is the words of music separated from their music. In the beginning was music.

The Lord of the Rings is full of singing. One of its indices lists fifty-six songs or poems. The Hobbits sing high hymns to Elbereth and homespun Walking Songs and Bath Songs. Tolkien, like Bombadil, is a writer of prose who is bursting with poetry and music. Peter Beagle calls him "a writer whose own prose is itself taut with poetry".[5]

Music is an essential part of Elvish enchantment. When the Fellowship enters Lothlorien, Sam says, "I feel as if I was *inside* a song, if you take my meaning" (LOTR, p. 342). And we say the same when we enter *The Lord of the Rings*.

The last division of philosophy that will ever be understood clearly and adequately by reason is aesthetics, and within aesthetics, music.

[5] J. R. R. Tolkien, *The Tolkien Reader* (New York: Ballantine Books, 1966), Foreword: "Tolkien's Magic Ring", p. xv.

10

Political Philosophy

Of all the divisions of philosophy, this is the one Tolkien was the *least* interested in. That is one of the typical differences between conservatives and progressives. In fact, one of his primary political convictions ("small is beautiful", or "populism") is by definition the antithesis of politics in the modern sense of something specialized, overarching, comprehensive, organized, bureaucratic, governmental, statist, socialist, and elitist.

10.1 Is small beautiful?

In general cultural terms, Tolkien is certainly a traditionalist, an antiprogressive, and an antimodernist. In political terms, is he also a "conservative" versus a "liberal"?

Yes and no. These two labels change with time, place, culture, and fashion, and Tolkien would probably be not much more comfortable with the American brand of conservatism, with its tendency to side with big business and the military and to ignore the poor and the environment, than he would with the American brand of liberalism, with its tendency to side with big government and ignore tradition, religion, morality, family, and the sacredness of individual human life. He is more of a European conservative, or old conservative, a Schumacher *Small is Beautiful* conservative, a

Chestertonian distributist. The Hobbits are certainly quintessentially "bourgeois" (the spit word for the Left, as "alcohol" is to pious Muslims). But they are not Babbitts, only peasants.

We could almost call Tolkien an anarchist as well as a monarchist: "My political opinions lean more and more to Anarchy (philosophically understood, meaning abolition of control not whiskered men with bombs)—or to 'unconstitutional' Monarchy" (*Letters*, no. 52, p. 63).

Anarchists are not usually patriots—but Tolkien was. And the reason was instinctive. It was because his country was to him not an ideological abstraction but a kind of extension of his concrete family, or at least of his pious mother, who, he wrote, "was a martyr indeed . . . a mother who killed herself with labour and trouble to ensure us keeping the faith." [1]

> Clichés about the influence of devout mothers do not begin to describe the force of an inheritance like this. . . . Chesterton was fond of quoting Cobbett on England's loss of medieval Catholicism through the Reformation as resembling one's discovery of one's mother's corpse in a wood. . . . To this extent there is an analogy with Irish Catholic nationalism. . . . Not only had Christ died for you: so had your country. . . . Tolkien, writing of his mother's martyrdom, would have felt much as Irish Catholics had. . . . Tolkien had seen his mother dying for his soul with his own eyes (ibid.).

Tolkien's political philosophy had a name: distributism. The term and the concept came from G. K. Chesterton and Hilaire Belloc. [2]

---

[1] *The Chesterton Review*, vol. 28, nos. 1 and 2 (Feb./May 2002), p. 58.
[2] See especially Belloc's *The Servile State* (New York: H. Holt and Company, 1946).

C. S. Lewis, who also admired this populist, libertarian philosophy, summed it up this way:

> I believe man is happier, and happy in a richer way, if he has "the free-born mind." But I doubt whether he can have this without economic independence, which the new society is abolishing. For economic independence allows an education not controlled by Government; and in adult life it is the man who needs, and asks, nothing of the Government who can criticize its acts and snap his fingers at its ideology. . . . Who will talk like that when the State is everyone's schoolmaster and employer? Admittedly, when man was untamed, such liberty belonged only to the few. I know. Hence the horrible suspicion that our only choice is between societies with few freemen and societies with none.[3]

And that is precisely the problem distributism claims to solve, by maximizing the distribution of private property.

This populism is not egalitarianism, however. Egalitarianism is an ism, an ideology. And every ideology leaves out something. Men differ in talents, so there are natural hierarchies as well as unnatural and oppressive hierarchies. Tolkien is not opposed to hierarchy ("unconstitutional" monarchy) and knows that much of our opposition to it comes from envy. Saruman embodies this and reveals it as his deeper motive when he tries to "sell" Gandalf his program of joining with Sauron: "In time, no one will stand higher than ourselves." (What he really means, of course, is that "no one will stand higher than I.")

Tolkien's patriotic populism also embraced an individualistic, or libertarian, tendency at odds with the totalitarianizing tendency of modernity, as did C. S. Lewis: "Two world wars

---

[3] "Willing Slaves of the Welfare State", in *C. S. Lewis: Essay Collection*, p. 338.

necessitated vast curtailments of liberty, and we have grown, though grumblingly, accustomed to our chains. . . . We are tamed animals . . . and should probably starve if we got out of our cage."[4]

> We have on the one hand a desperate need: hunger, sickness and the dread of war. We have, on the other, the conception of something that might meet it: omnicompetent global technocracy. Are not these the ideal opportunity for enslavement? . . .
>
> Let us not be deceived by phrases about "Man taking charge of his own destiny." All that can really happen is that some men will take charge of the destiny of the others. They will be simply men; none perfect; some greedy, cruel and dishonest. The more completely we are planned the more powerful they will be. Have we discovered some new reason why, this time, power should not corrupt as it has done before? (ibid., pp. 342–43).

Or, as Tolkien himself put it, "the proper study of Man is anything but Man; and the most improper job of any man . . . is bossing other men. Not one in a million is fit for it, and least of all those who seek the opportunity" (*Letters*, no. 52, p. 64).

Tolkien's myth of the Ring is not an allegory, but it is utterly "applicable". He says, "I think that many confuse 'applicability' with 'allegory'; but the one resides in the freedom of the reader, the other in the purposed domination of the author" (LOTR, p. xvii). Thus we are free to "apply" the concept of the Ring of power to many things and persons in our own age.

Some of these are obvious, by hindsight: Hitler, Stalin, Mao. But if we are astute enough to understand the warning

---

[4] Ibid., p. 340.

that there is a "soft totalitarianism" as well as a "hard totali-
tarianism", a *Brave New World* as well as a *1984*, we will thank
Tolkien for the ability to recognize in new forms the same
old "one Ring to rule them all, one Ring to find them, one
Ring to bring them all and in the darkness bind them". And
we may even apply the wisdom we have learned from *The
Lord of the Rings* to our own versions of "The Scouring of the
Shire", if any Shires still remain. Political action cannot keep
Middle-earth safe for Elves, but it can still keep it safe for
Hobbits.

10.2 Can war be noble?

War has always been that function of the State which touches
individual human lives most radically. War is literally a matter
of life or death. It is the art of killing those who want to kill
you—but on a collective scale. Only a State can wage a war.
When an individual kills on his own authority, it is called
murder.

The two simplest philosophies of war are, of course, pacifism and militarism. Pacifism demonizes war, militarism glorifies it. These are the two easy and obvious philosophies of
war, and they are as simplistic as are optimism and pessimism
in answering to the problem of whether man is by nature
good or evil. Tolkien accepts neither. He subscribes to the
traditional Just War Theory, which takes a middle road. It is
not a moral compromise; it is just as moralistic, as idealistic,
and as absolutistic, as pacifism or militarism. It does *not*
believe that "the end justifies the means", or that "all's fair in
love and war."

Faramir expresses Tolkien's philosophy of war perfectly
when he says to Frodo concerning the Ring:

"I would not take this thing, if it lay by the highway. Not were Minas Tirith falling in ruin and I alone could save her, so, using the weapon of the Dark Lord for her good and my glory. No, I do not wish for such triumphs.". . .

"I would see . . . Minas Tirith in peace: Minas Anor again as of old, full of light, high and fair, beautiful as a queen among other queens: not a mistress of many slaves, nay, not even a kind mistress of willing slaves. War must be, while we defend our lives against a destroyer who would devour all; but I do not love the bright sword for its sharpness, nor the arrow for its swiftness, nor the warrior for his glory. I love only that which they defend: the city of the Men of Numenor; and I would have her loved for her memory, her ancientry, her beauty, and her present wisdom. Not feared, save as men may fear the dignity of a man, old and wise" (LOTR, p. 656).

But this philosophy was apparently incomprehensible to the movie makers. Why else would they gratuitously change Faramir from heroic, honorable medieval knight to suspicious, uncertain fool who kidnaps Frodo and the Ring (at least temporarily)? This was the movie's single most substantial change in Tolkien's text.

Tolkien's distinctive contribution to the philosophy of war consists not just in the fairly common achievement of avoiding the two extremes of pacifism and militarism, but in the uncommon achievement of restoring the sense of the glory of a just war. It is not just a dirty job, or an unfortunate duty, it is a glorious thing. It is hard for most of us to feel, with the Roman poet, that "it is a sweet and just thing to die for your country" (*dulce et decorum est pro patria mori*). But it is hard *not* to feel your heart leap with joy at Theoden's transformation into a warrior and his "last battle" ride with the Rohirrim to save Gondor:

Theoden could not be overtaken. Fey he seemed, or the battle-fury of his fathers ran like new fire in his veins, and he was borne up on Snowmane like a god of old, even as Orome the Great in the battle of the Valar when the world was young. His golden shield was uncovered, and lo! It shone like an image of the Sun, and the grass flamed into green about the white feet of his steed. For morning came, morning and a wind from the sea; and darkness was removed, and the hosts of Mordor wailed, and terror took them, and they fled, and died, and the hoofs of wrath rode over them. And then all the host of Rohan burst into song, and they sang as they slew, for the joy of battle was on them, and the sound of their singing that was fair and terrible came even to the City (LOTR, p. 820).

As Lewis says in *Mere Christianity*, for the ancients a just war could be glorious, but for us moderns it is just a necessary dirty job, like cleaning toilets:

The idea of the knight—the Christian in arms for the defense of a good cause—is one of the great Christian ideas. War is a dreadful thing, and I can respect an honest pacifist, though I think he is entirely mistaken. What I cannot understand is this sort of semipacifism you get nowadays which gives people the idea that though you have to fight, you ought to do it with a long face and as if you were ashamed of it. . . . I have often thought to myself how it would have been if, when I served in the first world war, I and some young German had killed each other simultaneously and found ourselves together a moment after death. I cannot imagine that either of us would have felt any resentment or even any embarrassment. I think we might have laughed over it (*Mere Christianity*, p. 107).

The ultimate reason for the loss of this vision is cosmological: we have lost (but Lewis has not) the ancient vision of St. John in the Book of Revelation and St. Augustine in *The City of God*, that war on earth is always a manifestation of war in Heaven. The war between Sauron and Gandalf is a battle within the older and greater war between Melkor and Iluvatar.

Yet Tolkien believes there is a proper and honorable place for pacifists even in wartime. He explicitly says so when discussing Tom Bombadil, whom he labels both a contemplative (rather like a monk or mystic) and a pacifist:

> He represents something important. . . . It is a natural pacifist view, which always arises in the mind when there is a war. But the view of Rivendell seems to be that it is an excellent thing to have represented, but there are in fact things with which it cannot cope: and upon which its existence depends. Ultimately only the victory of the West will allow Bombadil to continue, or even to survive (*Letters*, no. 144, pp. 178–79).

Notice the difference between this "natural pacifist view" for special cases, like monks and mystics (and Bombadil), and ideological pacifism as a universal moral obligation.

C. S. Lewis's "Why I Am Not a Pacifist", a talk to the Pacifist Society, summarizes Tolkien's philosophy of war as well as his own. His two most potent arguments seem to be the following, the first being one of fact and the second one of religious principle:

> The main contention urged as fact by pacifists would be that wars always do more harm than good. . . . "Wars do no good" involves the proposition that if the Greeks had yielded to Xerxes and the Romans to Hannibal, the course of history ever since would have been perhaps

better, but certainly no worse than it actually has been; that a Mediterranean world in which Carthaginian power succeeded Persian would have been at least as good and happy and as fruitful for all posterity as the actual Mediterranean world in which Roman power succeeded Greek. ... On the test of the fact, then, I find the Pacifist position weak. It seems to me that history is full of useful wars as well as of useless wars. ...

It is arguable that a criminal can always be satisfactorily dealt with without the death penalty. It is certain that a whole nation cannot be prevented from taking what it wants except by war. ... [Pacifism] seems to imply a materialist ethic, a belief that death and pain are the greatest evils. But I do not think they are. I think the suppression of a higher religion by a lower, or even a higher secular culture by a lower, a much greater evil. ... Of course war is a very great evil. But that is not the question. The question is whether war is the greatest evil in the world, so that any state of affairs which might result from submission is certainly preferable. And I do not see any really cogent arguments for that view. ...

The whole Christian case for Pacifism rests on . . . utterances such as "Resist not evil; but whosoever shall smite thee on thy right cheek, turn to him the other also." . . . I think the text means exactly what it says. . . . No quarter whatever is given to the voice within us which says, "He's done it to me, so I'll do the same to him." But the moment you introduce other factors, of course, the problem is altered. Does anyone suppose that Our Lord's hearers understood Him to mean that if a homicidal maniac, attempting to murder a third party, tried to knock me out of the way, I must stand aside and let him get his victim? . . . Indeed, as the audience were private people in a disarmed nation, it seems unlikely that they would have ever supposed Our Lord to be referring to war. War was not what they would have been thinking of. The frictions of daily life among villagers were more likely to be in their minds. . . .

St. Paul approves of the magistrate's use of the sword (Romans 13:4) and so does St. Peter (I Peter 2:14). If Our Lord's words are taken in that unqualified sense which the Pacifist demands, we shall then be forced to the conclusion that Christ's true meaning, concealed from those who lived in the same time and spoke the same language, and whom He Himself chose to be His messengers to the world, as well as from all their successors, has at last been discovered in our own time.[5]

[5] "Why I Am Not a Pacifist", in *Weight of Glory*, pp. 39–41, 43, 48, 49–51.

11

Ethics: The War of Good and Evil

Ethics is certainly the most practically important division of philosophy, and the one most people think of first. But the most important part of ethics is not the one most people think of first. It is not the ethics of war, or sex, or money, or technology. It is not the ethics *of* anything but the foundations of ethics. Foundations are the most important part of any building, as roots to a tree. We thus first turn to what might be called "the metaphysical foundations of morality".

Morality is like the marching orders in the war between good and evil. Tolkien and Lewis strongly side with the traditional "natural moral law" view that this war, this distinction, and this goodness are objectively real. But is evil also objectively real, and, if so, is it equally real and equally powerful compared to good?

11.1 Is evil real?

Tolkien's classical Christian theology avoids two opposite errors, two oversimplifications. One is a Rousseauian optimism: the denial, or ignoring, of evil's reality and power, and consequently a kind of spiritual pacifism, the denial of spiritual warfare. The other would be the Manichean error, the idea that evil has the same kind of reality as goodness, equally powerful and equally substantial—in fact, that evil is, in the last analysis, a second God, or an equal, dark "side" of

God, as Shiva the Destroyer is forever equal to Vishnu the Preserver.

For half a century our culture has been as embarrassed by words like "sin", "wickedness", and "evil" as a teenager is embarrassed at being seen with his parents in a mall.

Some of our Deep Thinkers think that evil is only a temporary evolutionary stage, a hangover from ancient barbarisms of race, class, or gender that we will grow out of as we grow out of diapers. We are still waiting for the toilet training to take place.

Others say that evil is just ignorance, and therefore curable by education. After a century of universal education, we are still waiting for the cure to take. A study of which Nazis were most willing to kill Jews in Hitler's death camps revealed that this evil was indeed related to education, but not in the way expected: the more educated they were, the more willing they were.

Some say that evil against others is only the acting out of a lack of positive self-esteem. So Hitler did not esteem himself *enough*.

Most of our culture actually admires F.D.R.'s famous nonsense that "we have nothing to fear but fear itself." It sounds somehow healthy and even pious.

And then we saw the events of 9/11. In the chorus of voices that filled our media for the next few months, one was conspicuously silent from the babble: psychobabble. Where had all the gurus gone?

Tolkien's Christian theology told him that since the good God is the only creator of all beings, therefore all beings are ontologically good. But that theology also told him that God had given man free will and man had fallen into sin, which corrupts goodness and therefore corrupts beings (since being is the place where goodness can be found). Finally, his theology also told him that a man may, through evil choices, go to Hell, where he is hopelessly and forever evil.

The first of these three doctrines—ontological goodness—grounds Tolkien's "optimistic" cosmology; the other two—man's sinfulness and the reality of Hell—ground his "pessimistic" psychology. Both are shocks to secular philosophies: How can mud, mosquitoes, and even hemorrhoids be good, and how can we be so bad?

Yet, though he takes evil very seriously, Tolkien is not a pessimist, even about human nature. In fact, it is his moral optimism, his faith and hope in divine grace and in the triumph of good over evil, that deeply offends the modern secular critic. These critics label the heroes of *The Lord of the Rings* as simplistically moral, yet the antiheroes of most modern novels are much more simplistically immoral or amoral. It is the critics who are one-sided; Tolkien sees both the good and the evil sides better and deeper than they do. He is like a giant with both arms outstretched, one into the heights and the other into the depths. He scandalizes some small, simplistic souls by his glimpses of Heaven and others by his glimpses of Hell.

Think of the first time you saw the spectacular images of September 11. Now, remember not the images outside but the feeling inside. It was a sudden change from a peacetime consciousness to a wartime consciousness. It was a lot like the change from sleeping consciousness to waking consciousness, which your alarm clock triggers in you each morning. It was a sudden light, a sudden enlightenment. The world you woke up to was not brought into being by your waking up; it was always there. But *you* were not always there. You were dreaming. God sent prophets to wake you up, like alarm clocks.

That vision of life as a spiritual warfare between good and evil is the vision of life presupposed in every great story. For any great story must take both good and evil very seriously in order to generate great drama; and the fundamental theme of every great story is always this spiritual warfare between some particular good and some particular evil. The conflict between good and evil is the source of all conflict between characters. The source of all external conflict between characters is the internal conflict between good and evil *within* each character.

But Tolkien is not a Manichee: this war is not between equally powerful powers. It is not even between equally *real* powers. It requires a little philosophical clarification to make this point clear.

Good and evil are not equally powerful, because they are not equally real—even though evil *appears* not only equal to good but even *stronger* than good ("I am Gandalf, Gandalf the White, but Black is mightier still"). But appearance and reality do not coincide here, and in the end evil will always reveal its inevitable self-destruction (although often after a terrible price is paid: e.g., Napoleon, Hitler, Stalin). The self-destruction of evil is not just something to believe in and hope for, but to be certain of. It is metaphysically necessary, necessary because of the very kind of being evil has by its unchangeable essence. For evil can only be a parasite on good. It depends on a good host for it to pervert. "Nothing is evil in the beginning" or by nature: Morgoth was one of the Ainur, Sauron was a Maia, Saruman was the head of Gandalf's order of Wizards, the Orcs were Elves, the Ringwraiths were great Men, and Gollum was a Hobbit. And whenever a parasite succeeds in killing its host, it also kills itself. So if evil succeeds, it fails; it commits suicide.

The philosophical argument for evil being a parasite on good is simple: evil can exist only in some being, and all being is ontologically good, good for something, desirable somehow. Evil is the perversion of some version, the unnatural twisting of some nature; and all nature is good.

The argument for all being being good, in turn, is simply that "good" means "desirable", and everything real is desirable for something. Even the murderer's shot must be a good shot; moral evil can happen only by using ontological goodness.

The theological argument for the same conclusion is that every being is either the good God or a creature of this good God Who, being totally good, cannot will or create anything evil (though He can allow it, for a greater good, as He allows human sin in order to preserve human free will).

Yet though evil is not as real as goodness, it is real, terribly real; and life is spiritual warfare—there are snakes in the grass. And they come not just from the next yard. They come not from earth but from Hell. "For we are not contending against flesh and blood, but against the principalities, against the powers" (Eph 6:12). You do not need to commit the sin of allegory to see who the Black Riders are: "'They come from Mordor,' said Strider in a low voice. 'From Mordor, Barliman, if that means anything to you'" (LOTR, p. 165). Strider's laconic: "They are terrible!" (LOTR, p. 162) is more suggestive than any detailed description could be.

More evils come from Mordor than we think. "All those arts and subtle devices for which he [Saruman] forsook his former wisdom, and which fondly he imagined were his own, came but from Mordor" (LOTR, p. 542). And so did the little local evils in the Shire that had to be "scoured":

> "This is worse than Mordor!" said Sam. "Much worse in a way. It comes home to you, as they say, because it *is* home, and you remember it before it was all ruined."
>
> "Yes, this is Mordor," said Frodo. "Just one of its works" (LOTR, p. 994).

Tolkien certainly believes in the goodness of goodness and the badness of badness. He is not a moral relativist. But that does not make him a legalist or a fundamentalist. A common but indefensible error of some critics is to see *The Lord of the Rings* as morally "simplistic", as a "white versus black, good guys versus bad guys" story. This is so far from the truth as to be literally absurd. With the exception of Tom Bombadil, there is hardly a character in *The Lord of the Rings* who is not tempted by evil. The war is not just external, between the white chess pieces and the black, but within every single piece on the board, even while there is an external war going on between two sides that really but imperfectly represent the good (the Fellowship) and the evil (Mordor). Tolkien certainly would approve Solzhenitsyn's famous remark about the line between Good and Evil not dividing nations or cultures or ideologies but running through the middle of every human heart.

Tolkien is not a psychological absolutist but a moral absolutist: no person is absolutely good or evil; but goodness and evil themselves are absolutely distinct. He believes that "there's a little good in the worst of us and a little bad in the best of us"; but *not* that there's a little good in evil and a little evil in good. He believes in human moral complexity but not in logical moral complexity. He believes in the law of non-contradiction, in the goodness of goodness and the badness of badness. If that is his offense in the eyes of the critics, that tells us little about Tolkien but much about the critics.

Indeed, moral doubleness or "relativism" in the concrete does not contradict, but presupposes, moral singleness or absolutism in the abstract. If good and evil are not objectively real and absolutely distinct essences in the abstract, then the judgment that a concrete character is partly good and partly evil becomes meaningless.

Tolkien's moral absolutism contradicts the worldview of modern post-Christian moral relativism. But it also contradicts the pagan pre-Christian religious relativism. To see this, consider Tolkien's primary pagan source, Norse mythology. Odin, their supreme god, is not morally good, like the God of the Bible. He is addicted to power, like Sauron. The Vikings would never have understood the philosophy that "power corrupts." In fact, all the pagan gods, Northern (Germanic) or Southern (Mediterranean) are, like us, partly good and partly evil. They are "divine", or superior, not in goodness but only in power—in fact, in three powers: power over nature by a supernatural or "magical" technology, power over ignorance (cleverness, farsight and foresight), and power over death (immortality). (Exactly modernity's superiority over the past! If that is all divinity means, we are now approaching divinity.) The Jewish and Christian claim that the one God is totally good and not evil was as much of a shock to the old paganism as it is to the new.

11.2 How powerful is evil?

Evil is formidable. Its power shocks us. We are surprised to hear Gandalf say, "I am Gandalf, Gandalf the White, but Black is mightier still" (LOTR, p. 489). And, from the same Gandalf, after the great victory in the Battle of the Pelennor Fields, these words:

> "Against the Power that has now arisen there is no victory. . . .
> "Hardly has our strength sufficed to beat off the first great assault. The next will be greater. This war then is without final hope, as Denethor perceived. Victory cannot be achieved by arms. . . . I still hope for victory, but not by arms" (LOTR, p. 860).

Evil is in fact immortal, since Satan is immortal. Like Ransom in *Perelandra*, we can defeat only the temporary bodily forms that evil uses, the Un-men or Nazgul or Orcs or evil Wizards. We can break the swords but not the Swordsman. Only One can bruise his head, and only by being bruised in His heel.

All our victories against evil in this world are only temporary. The idea of progress, central to modernity, is simply false. We have not progressed in virtue or wisdom, only in power and cleverness. Good and evil are like odd and even integers; science and technology are only their exponents. They multiply whatever they are given, good or evil, odd or even.

The Ring is so powerful that no creature can overcome it. (Similarly, Christianity teaches that sin is so powerful that no creature can overcome it. Only God can, and only by His own death.)

> If the Ring represents Sin, then we would expect that its destruction would be impossible without the help of grace, and that is indeed what we find in *The Lord of the Rings*. . . . Frodo is, of course, saved by an apparent accident, for Gollum bites the Ring from his finger and falls into the Fire. This is in fact the consequence of Frodo's earlier (and freer) decision to spare Gollum's life. . . . Thus in the end it is not Frodo who saves Middle Earth at all, nor Gollum. It can only be God himself, working through the love and freedom of his creatures. The scene is a triumph of Providence over Evil but also a triumph of Mercy.[1]

Let us explore the power of evil more exactly. The Ring has two powers: it enhances whatever natural powers its user

---

[1] Stratford Caldecott, "The Horns of Hope", in *The Chesterton Review*, vol. 28, nos. 1 and 2 (Feb./May 2002), p. 37.

already has, and it gives him the new power of invisibility. What is the connection between these two powers? If you need deception to be powerful, then you need invisibility. If the Ring gave you power *without* invisibility, your evil would be known, and you would be caught and punished by having your power taken away. So the power of deception, which is over others' *minds* (symbolized by the invisibility given by the Ring), is an essential complement to the power over others' *bodies* and lives and actions, which is also given by the Ring. Machiavelli and Hitler both understood that principle; that's why they knew that propaganda was an essential part of war. The evil empire that controls modern world media knows that too, though its aim is not political conquest (like Machiavelli) or military conquest (like Hitler) but the far more apocalyptic spiritual and religious conquest of conscience, of souls.

Invisibility also means isolation. God alone can endure this (and only because He is a Trinity of persons, a society in Himself). He is God alone; there is no other. Yet He is other in Himself and never alone. God *is* a community. That is why He needs no community, as we do.

The Ring cuts us off from community, and contact. We are alone with the Eye. There is no room for two I's. There is no We in the I, no room for an Other in the One Ring.

This is why the Ring surrounds emptiness. If We-ness, or Relationship, or Love, or Trinity is the name of ultimate reality, then the Ring makes us unreal by isolating us. It plunges us into its own emptiness, like a Black Hole. Its circular shape is an image of that emptiness: it encloses nothingness with its all-encompassing circle of power.

It is not a means to any further end. It is Nietzsche's "will to power" as itself the end. Machiavelli taught that the end justified the means; Nietzsche taught that the means (power) justified the end. Nietzsche's nihilism is more demonic than Machiavelli's pragmatism. This philosophy sees life as a bubble: empty and meaningless within and without; its only meaning is to expand its own inner emptiness out into the outer emptiness, to make all Middle-earth into itself, into Mordor. It is the Worm Orouboros, swallowing its own tail, being its own god. It is the unholy icon of the inner life of Satan made visible.

Thus it images the very essence of sin, the first sin, Satan's sin: "Better to rule in Hell than serve in Heaven." And when Satan tempted Adam (Man, us) with it, Adam too tried to become invisible to God, to hide from the light, to give excuses and pass the blame to the woman, and she to the Devil.

The Ring symbol goes back to Plato, and probably even beyond him. In Plato's *Republic* we find the same Ring, with the same two powers. Or rather, Gyges does. (Gollum has many echoes of Gyges.) Gyges is a little man but the Ring makes him big. He is able to do anything he wants with impunity, since the Ring makes him invisible. So he murders the king, marries the queen, inherits the kingdom, and fools the people. Is he happy? That is the dramatic question of the *Republic*. It gives us the answer in the abstract; *The Lord of the Rings* gives us the same answer to the same question in the concrete.

Plato uses the Ring as the perfect contrast to Socrates, his Hobbit-like, Frodo-like model for the wise and humble and therefore happy life. Socrates has virtue in his soul, refuses to sell any of it for political power or survival, and consequently is martyred by evil men to whom his inner goodness is invisible. Socrates has the reality of goodness without the appearances of it or the rewards of it. Gyges, on the other hand, has no real goodness, no virtue, but through using the

Ring he gets what he wants, which includes apparent goodness and others' approval. For him, "Image is everything." His injustice is invisible to others; he controls appearances. And thus he is an apparent success. For, as Machiavelli argues, "Appearances are more important than reality for the successful prince. For you alone see what you really are, while everyone sees what you appear to be." In contrast, Socrates is a "failure"—like Christ. Like Frodo. Frodo is indeed a "Christ figure". As Plato used the Ring to contrast Gyges with Socrates, Tolkien uses the same Ring to contrast Gollum with Frodo, and, ultimately, with Christ.

Plato's great challenge to us in the *Republic* is this: Why should we be good if we can get whatever we want by being evil if we use the Ring of power and remain invisible and unpunished? And his answer is that wanting what you should is better than getting what you want.

But doesn't power make you happy, if it is the power to get whatever you want? Isn't the only gap between us and happiness the gap of power? For if we are unhappy only because we do not get what we want, because we do not have the power to bridge the gap between desire and satisfaction, and if the Ring would give us that power, then it follows that the Ring would make us happy. Thus "injustice is more profitable than justice" if it has a Ring.

The philosophy is profoundly similar to that of Nietzsche's. Gollum is really a small version of Nietzsche's "Overman". Sauron is a big one. It is no accident that Nietzsche called his final summary of his philosophy "The Will to Power". Nor is it a mere coincidence that the artist he found most fascinating was Wagner, the author of that other artistic masterpiece that centers on the Ring—exactly the same Ring. Both Plato and Tolkien write their masterpieces precisely to refute this philosophy. The issue could not be more momentous: nothing less than the meaning of life, the road to happiness.

Evil and injustice seem to be the secret of happiness sometimes, for they seem to give us the power to attain our desires. What is missing in this philosophy, for Plato, is wisdom: the wisdom to know ourselves and our desires. The thief is a fool: he thinks he is a body, not a soul, and that he will be happy by spending stolen money, ignoring his conscience. Tolkien would agree with this, but he goes farther. He knows something else that is missing in this Nietzschean philosophy: the power of weakness, the thing Nietzsche despised the most, especially in Christianity. For Tolkien, as for the saints, strength manifests itself most powerfully not in grasping and using power but in renouncing it, mortifying desires, yielding, self-sacrifice, and martyrdom. "The greatest examples of the action of the spirit . . . are in *abnegation*" (*Letters*, no. 186, p. 246).

Plato's answer to Gyges was philosophy, the love of wisdom, abstract knowledge. Tolkien's answer to Nietzsche is sanctity, the sacrificial love of persons, concrete acts of charity. That is why it is sufficient for Plato to *prove* his point in the abstract (with great brilliance and accuracy, let it be added); but Tolkien must *show* it concretely in the story that we see as *our* story.

11.3 How weak is evil?

The weakness of evil is that it cannot conquer weakness. No matter how much power evil has, it is always defeated by the *free, loving renunciation* of power. It can be defeated in Middle-earth as it was on Calvary: by martyrdom. Scripture's image of the last battle between good and evil is a battle between two mythical beasts: *Arnion*, the meek little Lamb, and

Therion, the terrible dragon beast. And the Lamb overcomes the Beast by a secret weapon: His own blood.

Evil is limited to power; it cannot use weakness. It is limited to pride; it cannot use humility. It is limited to inflicting suffering and death; it cannot use suffering and death. It is limited to selfishness; it cannot use selflessness. But good can.

It takes selflessness to give birth, whether biologically or artistically. You let yourself be used as a birth canal, or as an instrument of divine inspiration. Evil cannot create, or give birth. For "nothing is evil in the beginning" (LOTR, p. 261). "Trolls are only counterfeits, made by the Enemy in the Great Darkness, in mockery of Ents, as Orcs were of Elves" (LOTR, p. 474). "The Shadow that bred them can only mock, it cannot make" (LOTR, p. 893).

Martin Luther conveys both evil's power and its weakness in his great hymn:

> For still our ancient foe
> Doth seek to work us woe.
> His craft and power are great
> And, armed with cruel hate,
> On earth is not his equal.

> Did we in our own strength confide,
> Our striving would be losing,
> Were not the right Man on our side,
> The Man of God's own choosing.
> Dost ask who that may be?
> Christ Jesus, it is He!
> Lord Sabaoth His name.
> From age to age the same
> And He must win the battle.

For though this world, with devils filled,
Should threaten to undo us,
We will not fear, for God has willed
His truth to triumph through us.
The prince of darkness grim,
We tremble not for him.
His rage we can endure.
For lo, his doom is sure.
One little word shall fell him.

That Word, above all earthly powers
—no thanks to them—abideth.
The Spirit and the gifts are ours
Through Him who with us sideth.
Let goods and kindred go,
This mortal life also.
The body they may kill;
God's truth abideth still.
His kingdom is forever.

And "in the end the Shadow was only a small and passing thing: there was light and beauty for ever beyond its reach" (LOTR, p. 901).

"Only a small and passing thing"? But this Shadow is Satan, the one who succeeded in killing God for three days! Who but a Christian could possibly plumb the depths of evil, and therefore, by hard-won right, of good—as in Corrie Ten Boom's shattering confession in *The Hiding Place* from the antechambers of Hitler's Mordor in Ravensbrook: "This darkness is very deep, but our God has gone deeper still. When you have been to Calvary, even Ravensbrook looks small."

One reason the powerful Ring makes you weak rather

than strong is terrifyingly relevant to our own lives, dependent as they are on our many smaller rings of technologies. (Are we sure there is no one ruling Ring behind them all?) Tolkien explains:

> The Ring of Sauron is only one of the various mythical treatments of the placing of one's life, or power, in some external object [technically, this is "fetishism"—note that it is nearly identical with technologism!], which is thus exposed to capture or destruction with disastrous results to oneself. If I were to "philosophize" this myth, or at least the Ring of Sauron, I should say it was a mythical way of representing the truth that *potency* if it is to be exercised, and produce results, has to be externalized and so as it were passes, to a greater or less degree, out of one's direct control. A man who wishes to exert "power" must have subjects, who are not himself. But he then depends on them (*Letters*, no. 211, p. 279).

This is an example of Hegel's famous "master–slave dialectic": the slave does not need or depend on his master, but the master needs and depends on his slave; therefore the master is really the slave to his slave or, rather, to his own need for his slave, while the slave is free.

We do not have slaves because we have substitutes for them: machines. The Industrial Revolution made slavery inefficient and unnecessary. But our addiction is the same whether the slaves are made of flesh, metal, or plastic. We have done exactly what Sauron did in forging the Ring. We have put our power into things in order to increase our power. And the result is, as everyone knows but no one admits, that we are now weak little wimps, Shelob's slaves, unable to survive a blow to the great spider of our technological network. We tremble before a nationwide electrical blackout or a global computer virus. Only hillbillies and Boy Scouts would

survive a nuclear war. In our drive for power we have deceived ourselves into thinking that we have become more
powerful when all the time we have been becoming less. We
are miserable little Nietzsches dreaming we are supermen. For
in gaining the world we have lost our selves.

Who dares tell such a "reactionary" truth today? Tolkien
does, like the little boy in "The Emperor's New Clothes".
And we can't help listening to the prophet when he says,
"You can't fight the Enemy with his own Ring without
turning into an Enemy; but unfortunately Gandalf's wisdom
seems long ago to have passed with him into the True West"
(*Letters*, no. 81, p. 94).

This is why we never see Sauren's face in *The Lord of the
Rings*. It is because we do not see our own. We have forged a
Ring. Ours is not the supernatural technology of Sauron's
magic but natural technology. But, though the means are
different, they serve the same end.

And the critics call this "escapist fantasy"!

11.4 How does evil work?

The most terrifying thing about the power of evil is that it is
not external but internal. It works only by our cooperation.
It removes our freedom, but only freely; we forge the bonds
of our slavery with the strength of our freedom. The Ring's
temptation, in one word, is "addiction". This is also how
Plato analyzed injustice and tyranny in the *Republic*: enslave-
ment to the master passion for power.

Freud was wrong; it is not pleasure but power that we
want most demandingly. Kierkegaard saw this and wrote, "If
I had a humble servant who, when I asked him for a glass of
water, brought me instead the world's costliest wines blended
in a chalice, I would fire him, to teach him that true pleasure

consists in getting my own way." [2] Pleasure is only the sugar
on the bait of power. Any addict knows that. "I've got to
have it" is his philosophy. Not I but It is the Master. Gollum
is believable because we know him; he is every drug addict.
In fact, he is every addict, which means every man. For we
are all addicted to something that we cannot part with that is
less than God.

We are weak because we no longer understand the power
of weakness; we no longer understand that the greatest
power is in self-abnegation, renunciation, and martyrdom.
Even Catholics no longer use words like "mortification" or
even "detachment". But our heart still understands this
power; that's why we recognize it when we meet it in
Tolkien, or Buddha, or Lao Tzu, even after our Christian
teachers stopped teaching it to us in the name of Jesus.

Tolkien makes clear the connection between addiction
and technology in the strategy of temptation. We scientific
magicians demand not only gratification but instant gratification.

> The Enemy, or those who have become like him, go in
> for "machinery"—with destructive and evil effects—be-
> cause "magicians" . . . use *magia* for their own power. . . .
> The basic motive for *magia* . . . is immediacy: speed, re-
> duction of labour, and reduction also to a minimum (or
> vanishing point) of the gap between the idea or desire and
> the result or effect . . . if you have command of abundant
> slave-labour or machinery (often only the same thing
> concealed) (*Letters*, no. 155, p. 200).

Self-righteousness and egotism are another part of the
temptation. Denethor is supposed to be Gondor's steward

[2] Søren Kierkegaard, *Either/Or*, ed. Robert Bretail (New York: Modern
Library, 1936), p. 34.

(caretaker, servant). But he identifies Gondor with himself;
when he despairs of victory for Gondor, he commits suicide.
Gandalf, in contrast, is the exact opposite of a suicide: he is a
martyr. He dies for his companions in the Mines of Moria.
Gandolf says to Denethor, "The rule of no realm is mine,
neither of Gondor or any other, great or small. But all
worthy things that are in peril as the world now stands, those
are my care. . . . For I also am a steward. Did you not know?"
(LOTR, pp. 741–42).

At the nadir of the moral world stands pride, usually
counted as the deadliest sin, the sin of Satan. Pride always
includes the self-deception of self-righteousness. The lowest
of all moral states believes it is the highest. The more this
wrong dominates you, the more passionately do you insist
that you are in the right. The weaker you *are*, under your
drug, the more powerful you *feel*. The manifestation of this
self-delusion and self-righteousness is self-destruction, literally: Denethor kills himself because he insists that he is right
and reality is wrong: "I would have things as they were all the
days of my life. . . . But if doom denies this to me, then I will
have *naught*" (LOTR, p. 836). This is the philosophy of pride:
my way or the highway, my will or nothing. It is the philosophy of the totally spoiled child. It is the philosophy of those
on their way to Hell. It is the unforgivable sin: impenitence.
It cannot be forgiven because it *will* not be forgiven. And it
will not be forgiven because it will not repent. It insists that
it cannot be wrong, that reality must be wrong, whenever it
and reality, desire and satisfaction, do not coincide.

The thing we want the most is life, and therefore the thing
we fear the most is death, so the temptation to have power
over even death is the greatest temptation. And that, according to Tolkien himself, is the central theme of *The Lord of the
Rings*: "death and the deathless". The false immortality that

the heroes must renounce comes from the false magic of the Ring, which is unlimited power and thus even the power over death. Power over death is the power to extend your present self and will indefinitely, not only into space (conquering all Middle-earth and the wills of all its inhabitants) but also into time (conquering even death). The Ring turns God's good gift of life into the object of an evil addiction.

The Ring, of course, gives only a false immortality—that of the Undead, the Nazgul—just as it gives a false power and a false magic, for ultimately the Ring is the false Christ, the Antichrist. He is the world's ultimate drug dealer.

12

Ethics: The "Hard" Virtues

Virtues can be classified in many ways. One way is "hard" versus "soft". Our ancestors were better at the "hard" ones, like courage, duty, honor, chastity, and obedience. We are better at the "soft" ones, like pity, mercy, sensitivity, and humility. We are shocked by their cruelty; they would be equally shocked by our laxity.

12.1 Do principles or consequences make an act good?

There are ten men in a lifeboat, starving. If they kill one man and eat his flesh, nine will live. If they do not, all ten will die. Which is the ethically right choice? This is the classic example that distinguishes an absolutistic ethic of duty from a relativistic ethic of utility ("the end justifies the means"). Other examples would be waging a preventive war, assassinating a dictator, or burning incense to Caesar and calling him a god so that your family will not be fed to the lions in the Coliseum. Does the end (in both senses of "consequences" and "motive") justify the means in these cases? Or are there absolute principles that must be obeyed no matter what the consequences? The two answers can be labeled utilitarianism versus principialism, or relativism versus absolutism.

The basic difference between the two answers lies in what justifies a moral choice. Is it obedience to principles that are *a priori*, there *before* the act? Or is it your estimation of the good and bad consequences caused by the act, that come *after* it, *a posteriori*? This can be illustrated by a diagram.

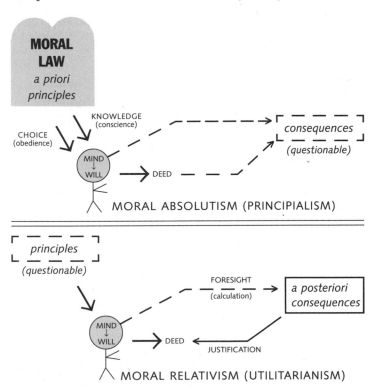

We find in *The Lord of the Rings* four arguments for principialism and against utilitarianism. They are implicit in the plot, of course, rather than explicitly argued, for Tolkien is not writing philosophy but story. But sometimes story's showing can be more convincing than philosophy's arguing.

There is, first, an epistemological argument. It is the simple fact that we do not know the future. We are not God.

Elrond's last words to the Fellowship (which his Council had chosen), as they exit Rivendell on their world-saving task, are: "You do not yet know the strength of your hearts, and you cannot foresee what each may meet upon the road. . . . Look not too far ahead" (LOTR, p. 274).

For these things change. But our marching orders, our principles, do not. They are unchanging and universal, not dependent on time or place. *And they are what we do know.* Tolkien never comes closer to summarizing his ethics than in Aragorn's reply to Eomer's question:

> "It is hard to be sure of anything among so many marvels. The world is all grown strange. Elf and Dwarf in company walk in our daily fields; and folk speak with the Lady of the Wood and yet live; and the Sword comes back to war that was broken in the long ages ere the fathers of our fathers rode into the Mark! How shall a man judge what to do in such times?"
>
> "As he ever has judged," said Aragorn. "Good and ill have not changed since yesteryear; nor are they one thing among Elves and Dwarves and another among Men. It is a man's part to discern them, as much in the Golden Wood as in his own house" (LOTR, pp. 427–28).

We know these principles, but not infallibly. We must *discern* them. And sometimes this is very hard, as in "The Choices of Master Samwise", when Sam thought Frodo had been killed by Shelob and could not clearly discern whether to take the Ring or to stay with his Master (LOTR, pp. 711–25).

Our reasoning is not always right and sometimes must be overridden by a deeper knowledge—thus Sam's interior dialogue on Mount Doom. His calculating voice says,

> "You are the fool, going on hoping and toiling. You could have lain down and gone to sleep together two days ago, if

you hadn't been so dogged. But you'll die just the same, or worse. You might just as well lie down now and give it up. You'll never get to the top anyway."

And then his deeper wisdom answers,

"I'll get there, if I leave everything but my bones behind," said Sam. "And I'll carry Mr. Frodo up myself, if it breaks my back and heart. So stop arguing!" (LOTR, p. 918).

Notice that Sam's deeper wisdom treats his rationalizing voice as an *other*, not as his self. What passes for reasoning is often rationalizing, and our deeper reason knows it. Moral absolutism is not arrogant but humble. It claims absolute status for principles, not for our knowledge of them. It is moral relativism that is arrogant, both because it will not bow to principles and because it plays God in assuming we can know the future, the consequences, like a soldier disobeying his orders because he thinks he knows better than his commanding officer.

A second argument for absolutism is an anthropological argument. Here again the difference is exactly the reverse of what the relativist claims. The relativist claims that his philosophy is personalistic and warm, designed to love and help people. After all, principles are for people, not vice versa. But in fact, as we shall see in the plot of *The Lord of the Rings*, the relativist's "flexibility" actually harms people rather than helping them, while the absolutist's adherence to principles helps people. So the real personalism is principialism. It is the utilitarian who will sacrifice persons if "necessary", like Saruman. The utilitarian ranks quantity over quality, and calculates that nine live cannibals in a lifeboat are better than ten dead heroes.

Principles are indeed for persons rather than vice versa: that's why they are so absolute, especially principles like

loyalty and friendship. Tolkien's heroes are certainly not un-
feeling legalists.

Duty is really to persons, not to principles. Frodo says, at
the Black Gate, "I am commanded to go to the land of
Mordor, and therefore I shall go. . . . If there is only one way,
then I must take it. What comes after must come" (LOTR, p.
624). (Note the last sentence. Tolkien is deliberately rejecting
utilitarianism with its calculation of consequences.) Like
Eowyn, Frodo has been "commanded", by a person, not a
principle. And he knows and trusts his commanders (Elrond
and Gandalf) and therefore obeys them. He does not say,
as Kant did, that he obeys reason, or duty, or the Categorical
Imperative. He does not say, "I think my rational duty is this,
and I obey *it*." Ultimately, obedience and duty come down to
knowing, trusting, and loving a person.

A third argument for absolutism is psychological. It is very
simple: bad people are often utilitarians. Utilitarianism
tempts you to badness; it is a very convenient excuse for
doing something bad. Thus Saruman's argument to Gandalf
(LOTR, p. 253) for joining the apparently inevitable winner,
Sauron, before it's too late. But good people are not utilitarians. Why? Because they exercise the great non-utilitarian
moral virtues: charity, self-forgetfulness, self-sacrifice:

> "Gandalf chose to come himself, and he was the first to be
> lost," answered Gimli. "His foresight failed him."
> "The counsel of Gandalf was not founded on fore-
> knowledge of safety, for himself or for others," said Ara-
> gorn (LOTR, p. 430).

Gandalf's counsel is the heart of Tolkien's ethics. It is short
and sweet, hard and true: "To cast aside regret and fear. To do
the deed at hand" (LOTR, p. 507).

A fourth argument for moral absolutism is a historical

one. It is an argument not from principles but from consequences. In fact, it is a consequentialist argument against consequentialism. It is that the consequences of consequentialism are bad, and the consequences of principialism are good.

Consequentialism gives up too easily. Frodo, seeing the vast army of Mordor, at first thinks, "I am too late. All is lost. I tarried on the way. All is lost. Even if my errand is performed, no one will ever know. There will be no one I can tell. It will be in vain." But, then, "Despair had not left him, but the weakness had passed. He even smiled grimly, feeling now as clearly as a moment before he had felt the opposite, that what he had to do, he had to do, if he could, and that whether Faramir or Aragorn or Elrond or Galadriel or Gandalf or anyone else ever knew about it was beside the purpose" (LOTR, p. 692).

C. S. Lewis defended moral absolutism and attacked utilitarianism in many places—for instance, in the first book of *Mere Christianity*; in one of the century's most prophetic books, *The Abolition of Man* (which is too long to quote but not too long to read); and in the shorter article "The Poison of Subjectivism".

One of the sharpest examples of the conflict between duty and utility in his fiction is Digory's choice in *The Magician's Nephew* to obey Aslan and not accept a magic apple from the Witch even though it would have healed his dying mother. Aslan tells him that

> it would have healed her, but not to your joy or hers. The day would have come when both you and she would have looked back and said it would have been better to die in that illness. . . . That is what *would* have happened, child, with a stolen apple. It is not what will happen now. What I give you now will bring joy. It will not, in your world,

give endless life, but it will heal. Go. Pluck her an apple from the Tree.[1]

Here, as in Tolkien, consequentialism has bad consequences and obedience to duty rather than consequences has good ones. It is the Principle of "First and Second Things" (see Lewis's essay by that title in God in the Dock).

12.2 Why must we be heroes?

A hero is a person who acts courageously. In a fallen world, courage is among the most important of virtues. Chesterton, musing on Gethsemane and Calvary, notes that Christianity is "the only religion which adds *courage* to the virtues of the Creator". Tolkien says, "The 'good' of the world depends on the behaviour of an individual in circumstances which demand of him suffering and endurance far beyond the normal . . . demand a strength of body and mind which he does not possess" (*Letters*, no. 181, p. 234).

A recent book on *The Lord of the Rings* notes that

a big part of the reason Frodo's courage is so inspiring is its contrast to his culture. His upbringing nurtured the pursuit of happy ease. . . . Have you ever wondered why our favorite stories tend to include an ordinary person overcoming great odds to accomplish something extraordinary? It's because the capacity and desire to be heroic resides deep within each of us . . . Rocky Balboa . . . Luke Skywalker . . . Forrest Gump . . . William Wallace . . . Gideon . . . Wilberforce . . . Rosa Parks.[2]

---

[1] C. S. Lewis, *The Magician's Nephew* (New York: Macmillan, 1970), p. 175.
[2] K. Bruno and J. Ware, *Finding God in The Lord of the Rings* (Wheaton, Ill.: Tyndale House, 2001), p. 39.

C. S. Lewis says of courage, "As Johnson points out, where courage is not, no other virtue can survive except by accident" (*Surprised by Joy*, p. 161). "Courage is not simply one of the virtues, but the form of every virtue at the testing point, which means, at the point of highest reality" (*The Screwtape Letters*, p. 148). Lewis points out that Jesus was not a man of great *natural* courage, as seen by Gethsemane. Neither was Tolkien, as seen by Letter 210. Jesus was like Frodo!

12.3 Can one go on without hope?

There are two kinds of hope, as there are two kinds of faith. One kind lives only on the conscious surface of the self, in the feelings and the mind. This kind often has to be killed in order for the deeper hope to emerge. The Fellowship often has to do without this surface hope, especially after the loss of Gandalf in Moria and when Frodo and Sam crawl through Mordor. But they continue to act, to fight, to give every ounce of themselves because of a deeper hope, which is much harder to identify or define. Let us look at these two kinds of hope in the text.

Nearly every time Tolkien uses the word, he means surface hope, and when it disappears, deep hope takes over and the result is not inaction or surrender but total commitment to battle and action.

After Gandalf's death in Moria, Aragorn, now in command, says:

> "Farewell, Gandalf!" . . . "Did I not say to you: *if you pass the doors of Moria, beware?* Alas that I spoke true! What hope have we without you?"
>
> He turned to the Company. "We must do without hope," he said (LOTR, p. 324).

When Frodo and Sam first approach the Black Gate, it seems absolutely hopeless to try to sneak in past thousands of Orcs. But Frodo's

> face was grim and set, but resolute. He was filthy, haggard, and pinched with weariness, but he cowered no longer, and his eyes were clear. ". . . I purpose to enter Mordor, and I know no other way. Therefore I shall go this way. I do not ask anyone to go with me."
> . . . Sam said nothing. The look on Frodo's face was enough for him; he knew that words of his were useless. And after all he never had any real hope in the affair from the beginning; but being a cheerful Hobbit he had not needed hope, as long as despair could be postponed. Now they were come to the bitter end. But he had stuck to his master all the way; that was what he had chiefly come for, and he would still stick to him. His master would not go to Mordor alone. Sam would go with him (LOTR, pp. 623–24).

An even more total despair settles upon the Fellowship outside the Black Gate. For it seems the whole Quest has failed and Frodo and the Ring have been captured when Sauron's messenger brings out Frodo's sword, cloak, brooch, and mithril mail-shirt. "A blackness came over their eyes, and it seemed to them in a moment of silence that the world stood still, but their hearts were dead and their last hope gone" (LOTR, p. 871). Yet they do not yield, but fight to the end. Pippin's last thought is: " 'So it ends as I guessed it would,' his thought said, even as it fluttered away; and it laughed a little within him ere it fled, almost gay it seemed to be casting off at last all doubt and care and fear" (LOTR, p. 874).

Frodo and Sam also lose hope, yet continue to act, when approaching Mount Doom. Frodo says to Sam, near the end,

"Lead me! As long as you've got any hope left. Mine is gone" (LOTR, p. 907).

"So that was the job I felt I had to do when I started," thought Sam; "to help Mr. Frodo to the last step and then die with him? Well, if that is the job then I must do it." . . . But even as hope died in Sam, or seemed to die, it was turned into a new strength. Sam's plain hobbit-face grew stern, almost grim, as the will hardened in him, and he felt through all his limbs a thrill, as if he was turning into some creature of stone and steel that neither despair nor weariness nor endless barren miles could subdue.

With a new sense of responsibility he brought his eyes back to the ground near at hand, studying the next move (LOTR, p. 913).

What is this deeper hope that emerges when all hope is gone? What is its object?

It is not a feeling of optimism, a Mister Micawber philosophy of "something will turn up." Quite the contrary. Galadriel warns Frodo, "[Y]our Quest stands upon the edge of a knife. Stray but a little, and it will fail, to the ruin of all" (LOTR, p. 348). That hardly sounds like optimism.

It is certainly not calculation, not utility. In fact, it arises only when calculation and utility fail. As Gabriel Marcel says, "While the structure of the world we live in permits—and may even seem to counsel—absolute despair, yet it is only such a world that can give rise to an unconquerable hope."[3] So its object is not the world as seen. Despair of that world seems to be the precondition for hope in the deeper sense.

But hope's object is not miracle, and not (at least not explicitly) another world that begins only after death, as a kind of compensation for loss in this one. In *this* world, as

<hr />

[3] Gabriel Marcel, "On the Ontological Mystery", in *The Philosophy of Existentialism* (New York: Citadel Press, 1959), p. 17.

Gandalf says, "The enemy is strong beyond our reckoning, yet we have a hope at which he has not guessed" (LOTR, p. 505).

Hope's object is *persons*, and their *emeth*, their trustworthiness, and the trust, loyalty, and friendship between them. At first the hope of the Fellowship is lodged in Gandalf—rightly, for he is really one of the Maiar, an archangel sent to this world only to combat Sauron, as he reveals at the end (LOTR, p. 950). Gandalf returns from death, like Christ, in the morning light (even the "Easter" date is noted: March 1). If anyone else but Gandalf had sent Frodo and Sam into Mordor on an apparently hopeless errand, no one could have had hope for the errand. Hope for the task depends on trust in the taskmaster.

Hope's object is always a person, not an idea or ideal, not even the fulfillment of the task. Frodo, in fact, loses hope in his task, but he still has hope in *Sam*. Sam never did have much hope for the task; the object of his deep hope is *Frodo*, and that hope is not disappointed. Even as they prepare to die on Mount Doom, he is happy because his master is free.

Hope's object is always personal, but it is never one's self. Hope in one's self is either foolish vanity or even more foolish pride. That is why even a mere thing is a surer sign of hope than a person if the thing is outside yourself and the person is yourself. Thus Sam's sighting of the star in Mordor is, for me, the most moving passage in the entire book:

> There, peeping among the cloud-wrack above a dark tor high up in the mountains Sam saw a white star twinkle for a while. The beauty of it smote his heart, as he looked up out of the forsaken land, and hope returned to him. For like a shaft, clear and cold, the thought pierced him that in the end the Shadow was only a small and passing thing:

there was light and high beauty for ever beyond its reach (LOTR, p. 901).

Hope is like the sky, unconquerable and spread over everything. Hope's object is not limited to particulars; it is universal, it is the nature of things, it is Being itself. Thus Marcel says,

> To hope against all hope that a person whom I love will recover from a disease which is said to be incurable is to say: It is impossible that I should be alone in willing this cure; it is impossible that reality in its inward depth should be hostile or so much as indifferent to what I assert is in itself a good. It is quite useless to tell me of discouraging *cases* or *examples*: beyond all experience, all probability, all statistics, I assert that a given order shall be established, that reality is on my side in willing it to be so. I do not wish: I assert; such is the prophetic tone of true hope (*Philosophy of Existentialism*, p. 17).

Since (1) hope's object is always in the last analysis a person, not an abstraction, and since (2) that object is also in the last analysis universal and not particular, it follows that (3) that object must always, at least implicitly and anonymously, be God, the only concrete universal, the only Person ("I") who is also Being ("AM").

Which brings us back to the traditional Christian labeling of hope as one of the three theological virtues, that is, God-oriented virtues. We do not enter a C. S. Lewis quotation on this topic here not because there is too little but because there is too much. This is Lewis's most distinctive theme, and in light of all that he has written about this: in his autobiography *Surprised by Joy*, in the "Heaven" chapter in *The Problem of Pain*, in the Introduction to *The Pilgrim's Regress*, in the "Hope" chapter in *Mere Christianity*, and in *The Weight of*

Glory, we need another whole book to begin to do it justice. I offer you my own very feeble attempt to do just that: *Heaven, the Heart's Deepest Longing* (San Francisco: Ignatius Press, 1981).

Instead, here is a single sentence from Lewis's autobiography, as a sort of test: "It is more important that Heaven should exist than that any of us should get there." If you understand this sentence (it may take years), you will understand three things about this deep hope: why it comes when other hope fails, why it is hope in what does not depend on yourself, and why it nevertheless does not lead you to resignation and passivity but steels you for action. All three effects flow from the same fact that, like charity, it de-centers you from yourself.

12.4 Is authority oppressive and obedience demeaning?

Frodo is a Marian figure. His *fiat* ("I will take the Ring though I do not know the way" [LOTR, p. 264]) is strikingly similar to Mary's ("Let it be to me according to your word" [Lk 1:38]). They are opposite sides of the same coin: Mary consented to carry the Savior of the whole world, the Christ, to birth, to life; and Frodo consented to carry the destroyer of the whole world, the Ring, the Antichrist, to its death. Mary gave life to Life (Christ); Frodo gave death to Death (the Ring).

We all, like Frodo, carry a Quest, a Task: our daily duties. They come *to* us, not from us. We are free only to accept or refuse our task—and, implicitly, our Taskmaster. None of us is a free creator or designer of his own life. "None of us lives to himself, and none of us dies to himself" (Rom 14:7). Either God, or fate, or meaningless chance has laid upon each of us a Task, a Quest, which we would not have chosen for ourselves. We are all Hobbits who love our Shire, our security, our creature comforts, whether these are pipeweed, mushrooms, five meals a day, and local gossip, or Starbucks coffees, recreational sex, and politics. But something, some authority not named in *The Lord of the Rings* (but named in *The Silmarillion*), has decreed that a Quest should interrupt this delightful Epicurean garden and send us on an odyssey. We are plucked out of our Hobbit holes and plunked down onto a Road. That gives us our fundamental choice between obedience and disobedience. And if life is war, obedience is essential. It is the first virtue for a soldier.

C. S. Lewis says that "obedience accepted with delight and authority exercised with humility are the very lines along which our spirits live" (*The Weight of Glory*, p. 115). And "If you ask why we should obey God, in the last resort the answer is, 'I am.' To know God is to know that our obedience is due to Him" (*Surprised by Joy*, p. 231). Like Frodo, Lewis believes in an ethic of duty and obedience rather than an ethic of consequences: "To play well the scenes in which we are 'on' concerns us much more than guessing about future scenes" (*The World's Last Night*, p. 104).

12.5 Are promises sacred?

This is a single concept, though there is not a single word for it in English. "Honesty" has been too often trivialized in modern parlance to mean mere candor, which is often only shamelessness, not a virtue but a vice. In Hebrew there *is* a single word, and it is *emeth* (truth), but the "truth" not only of a thought or even of a deed but of a person, or a person's character. It is one of the primary attributes of God in the Old Testament. It is manifested especially in keeping promises.

It can be seen best, perhaps, by contrasting two concrete characters: Faramir and Boromir. But we must simply forget, if not forgive, the movie's gratuitous redrawing of the character of Faramir as crafty and suspicious and lusting after the Ring. Rather, we must remember his noble words:

> "I would not snare even an Orc with a falsehood," said Faramir (LOTR, p. 949).

> "We are truth-speakers, we men of Gondor. We boast seldom, and then perform, or die in the attempt. *Not if I found it on the highway would I take it* I said. Even if I were such a man as to desire this thing, and even though I knew not clearly what this thing was when I spoke, still I should take those words as a vow, and be held by them" (LOTR, pp. 665–66).

Boromir, on the other hand, betrays his vow to the Fellowship to protect the Ring bearer when he succumbs to Ring lust and tries to lure Frodo into giving him the Ring, then tries to take it by force.

But Boromir is only stubborn and weak, and repents. The more complete lack of *emeth* is found in Gollum. (Perhaps the best character to contrast him with would be Emeth himself in C. S. Lewis's *The Last Battle*.) He has lost his soul, his "I", his integrity. He can no longer even use that sacred word, the word God revealed as His own eternal Name in the burning bush (see Ex 3:14). He speaks of himself in the plural ("we", "us") or in the third person ("They took his Precious and he's lost now" (LOTR, p. 602)—until Frodo binds him with a promise:

> "No, I will not take it [the Elf-rope] off you," said Frodo, "not unless"—he paused a moment in thought—"not

unless there is any promise you can make that I can trust."
  "We will swear to do what he wants, yes, yess," said
Gollum. . . . "We promises, yes I promise!" said Gollum. "I
will serve the master of the Precious" (LOTR, pp. 603–4).

The "I" and the "promise" necessarily go together.

How important are promises? Keeping them was the main
thing King Theoden was eulogized for: he "kept his oaths"
(LOTR, p. 851). When Aragorn took "the Paths of the Dead"
(really, the Undead) he roused them to fight and thus gave
them the rest they had been denied because they had broken
their oath to fight against Sauron:

> "Oathbreakers, why have ye come?"
>   And a voice was heard out of the night that answered
> him, as if from far away: "To fulfill our oath and have
> peace" (LOTR, p. 772).

Promise keeping is the fundamental thing that holds all
societies together. It is the root of all law and thus of all social
stability. Personal integrity is the basis for social integrity. All
pre-modern societies knew that. Tolkien notes that "promises were held sacred, and of old all but the wickedest things
feared to break them" (LOTR, p. 12).

The consequences of promise breaking are the loss of
personal integrity. And the consequences of that are
Gollum's inner Hell, which is the exact opposite of Sartre's in
No Exit, where "Hell is other people." Gollum's Hell is the
withdrawal from the other, as it is in Charles Williams's truly
terrifying *Descent Into Hell*.

The virtue of *Emeth* is the precondition for all virtue.
There can no more be any other virtue without truthfulness
than there can be any successful operation without light in
the operating room. Even moral relativists know this: no one
admires a man who lies to himself, who sins against his own

conscience. Even the wicked have this light, for it is the light that enlightens every man who comes into the world (see Jn 1:9). Without it, nothing.

And with it, everything. There is no more life-transforming reform than total honesty, the absolute refusal to lie to oneself or others. Ask anyone in A.A. That's why we need Purgatory, for our sins to come into the light. That's why "practicing the presence of God" and *momento mori* (remember death) is the way to sanctity: there are not many sins a man will commit on his deathbed.

C. S. Lewis was an absolutist about honesty, especially in "Man or Rabbit?" If Lewis could make everyone in our world read any one short essay or chapter he wrote, I think he would choose that one.

It begins with a question: "Can't you lead a good life without believing in Christianity?" And his answer is to question the question:

> The question sounds as if it were asked by a person who said to himself, "I don't care whether Christianity is in fact true or not. . . . All I'm interested in is leading a good life. I'm going to choose beliefs not because I think them true but because I find them helpful." Now frankly, I find it hard to sympathise with this state of mind. . . . If Christianity is untrue, then no honest man will want to believe it, however helpful it might be; if it is true, every honest man will want to believe it, even if it gives him no help at all.[4]

---

[4] "Man or Rabbit", in *God in the Dock*, pp. 108–9.

Ethics: The "Soft" Virtues

13.1 What is the power of friendship?

The importance of this topic to Tolkien is evident from the title of the first volume: *The* Fellowship *of the Ring*. "Fellowship" is another word for friendship.

It is a greater power than wisdom. Gandalf knows this, and that is why he picks Merry and Pippin at the Council of Elrond. "It is true that if these hobbits understood the danger, they would not dare to go. But . . . I think, Elrond, that in this matter it would be well to trust rather to their friendship than to great wisdom" (LOTR, p. 269).

This is why Gandalf is so happy to hear that Sam went with Frodo into Mordor after the Fellowship broke up at Amon Hen: a mini-fellowship, at least, might work, but a lone individual would not.

There is evidently a connection between this point, the value of friendship, and the previous one about the superiority of duty to utility, or calculation. Soldiers do not die for causes, or even for "country", but for their buddies, their friends. Friendship shows its power most when the situation is most desperate and temptation is strongest—as it was for Sam in the tower of Cirith Ungol. "In that hour of trial it was the love of his master that helped most to hold him firm" (LOTR, p. 881). Friendship, after all, is a form of love.

If there is one single thing that was most responsible for

the success of the Fellowship, it was their fellowship, their friendship, especially between Frodo and Sam. That literally carried the Ring to Mount Doom:

> "I said I'd carry him, if it broke my back," he muttered, "and I will!"
>
> "Come, Mr. Frodo!" he cried. "I can't carry it for you, but I can carry you and it as well. So up you get! Come on, Mr. Frodo dear! Sam will give you a ride. . . ."
>
> Sam staggered to his feet; and then to his amazement he felt the burden light. He had feared that he would have barely strength to lift his master alone, and beyond that he had expected to share in the dreadful dragging weight of the accursed Ring. But it was not so (LOTR, p. 919).

Of course not: "He ain't heavy; he's my brother."

In this Sam fulfilled to the letter his promise at the beginning:

> "It is going to be very dangerous, Sam. It is already dangerous. Most likely neither of us will come back."
>
> "If you don't come back, sir, then I shan't, that's certain," said Sam. *Don't you leave him!* They said to me. *Leave him!* I said. *I never mean to. I am going with him, if he climbs to the Moon, and if any of those Black Riders try to stop him, they'll have Sam Gamgee to reckon with,* I said (LOTR, p. 85).

And Merry and Pippin too: "You can trust us to stick to you through thick and thin—to the bitter end. . . . But you cannot trust us to let you face trouble alone, and go off without a word. We are your friends, Frodo" (LOTR, p. 103).

And because friendship is so close to the whole meaning of life, that is why it is self-sufficient, why its fruit is joy, even if everything else is lost. After Gollum fell into the Crack of Doom liberating Frodo from the Ring, Sam was totally happy, even though all other hopes seemed totally gone:

"Well, this is the end, Sam Gamgee," said a voice by his side. And there was Frodo, pale and worn, and yet himself again; and in his eyes there was peace now. . . .

"Master!" cried Sam, and fell upon his knees. In all that ruin of the world for the moment he felt only joy, great joy. The burden was gone. His master had been saved; he was himself again, he was free. . . .

"I'm glad you are here with me. Here at the end of all things, Sam" (LOTR, p. 926).

With-ness: that is all friendship wants. That is joy, because it is the image of what ultimate reality is if Tolkien's Christian faith is true. The pagan mystic may seek his joy in the flight of the alone to the Alone, but not the Christian. For according to that faith, the trinitarian God Who is not alone made man in His own image and declared that "it is not good for man to be alone", even in ruin.

It is because friendship, fellowship, and loyalty are so good that their opposites, treason and betrayal, are so bad. Gandalf knows that "In all the wars with the Dark Tower treason has ever been our greatest foe" (LOTR, p. 245). "Indeed in nothing is the power of the Dark Lord more clearly shown than in the estrangement that divides all those who still oppose him" (LOTR, p. 339). Satan's simplest strategy is "divide and conquer".

C. S. Lewis not only wrote great things about friendship (especially in the chapter devoted to that subject in *The Four Loves*) but practiced it. In fact, he was Tolkien's closest friend. But for his Churchillianly dogged encouragement, we would never have seen *The Lord of the Rings* in print.

He notes that "to the ancients, Friendship seemed the happiest and most fully human of all loves; the crown of life and the school of virtue. The modern world, in comparison, ignores it . . . very few modern people think Friendship . . . even a love at all" (*Four Loves*, p. 55).

Those who cannot conceive Friendship as a substantive love but only as a disguise or elaboration of Eros betray the fact that they have never had a friend. . . . In some ways nothing is less like a Friendship than a love-affair. Lovers are always talking to one another about their love; Friends hardly ever about their Friendship. Lovers are normally face to face, absorbed in each other; Friends, side by side, absorbed in some common interest [such as saving all of Middle-earth from Sauron and his Ring] (ibid., p. 58).

13.2 Is humility humiliating?

In *The Lord of the Rings* the Hobbits appear at first to be only comic contrast to the larger and more heroic Men and Elves; yet almost all the greatest deeds are achieved by Hobbits. Bilbo was instrumental in killing Smaug the Dragon in *The Hobbit*; Merry saves Eowyn and helps her slay the Lord of the Nazgul; Pippin helps save Faramir from Denethor; Merry and Pippin move the Ents to destroy Isengard; Sam wounds Shelob; and Frodo—"What more shall I say? For time would fail me to tell" (Heb 11:32). After many mighty little heroics along every step of the way, Frodo finally saves all of Middle-earth, with Gollum's unforeseen help, and destroys Sauron and his Ring. Not Gandalf or Aragorn or the Elves but Frodo achieves the Quest (and only by the help of Sam and Gollum). Not Aragorn but Frodo is taken to Heaven, like the wounded Arthur, at the end.

One of the main themes of *The Lord of the Rings* is the relation of mutual dependence between the high-heroic and the humble-Hobbit-like. The motive for the heroic is the defense of ordinary life: wars are fought, heroically, to protect ordinary peaceful non-heroes. Correlatively, the enjoyment of ordinary life (the Shire) is the reward for heroism, and only heroism can sustain it. This is a literary bridge that carries the reader's mind over it in both directions, a Jacob's Ladder on which the reader's thoughts continually ascend and descend between the low and earthly and the high and Heavenly.

Tolkien confesses of his Hobbits, "I loved them myself, since I love the vulgar and simple as dearly as the noble, and nothing moves my heart . . . so much as 'ennoblement' (from the Ugly Duckling to Frodo)" (*Letters*, no. 180, p. 232). Tolkien loves Hobbits so much that he writes an eight-page reply to a reader's question about who among the Hobbits gives and who receives birthday presents! (*Letters*, no. 214, p. 289).

He loves them so much that he loses many of his readers in the first fifty pages of utterly provincial details about the habits of Hobbits. Many of us who love *The Lord of the Rings* and have learned to love Hobbits must confess that the first time we read this book we were put off by the long, slow start and were tempted to give up before the "excitement" began. Many of us did.

Tolkien not only loves his Hobbits, he is one: "I am in fact a *Hobbit* (in all but size)" (*Letters*, no. 213, p. 288).

Among the Hobbits it is not even Frodo but Sam, the humble servant, who is the most heroic. Tolkien, several times in his letters, insists that Sam is "the chief hero" of *The Lord of the Rings*. But Sam at the beginning seems only a comic figure, and throughout the narrative his importance seems merely relative to Frodo, as Frodo's servant and gardener—by definition a secondary character. Very much in the style of the God he believes in, Tolkien raises up the lowly to put down the lordly. *The Lord of the Rings* is the perfect illustration of Mary's "Magnificat" (see Lk 1:46–55). (Work it out for yourself, verse by verse.)

Sam's exaltation into hero is believable because Sam is Sam, and not just servant. He is more than his role. There are fixed roles, and hierarchy, in his pre-modern society; yet there are also real individuals. (Perhaps we should say, "*Therefore* there are real individuals.") Sam has enough independence to conspire to go with Frodo out of the Shire and to stay with him when the Fellowship breaks up at Amon Hen, though both times Frodo tried to "escape". He is also more open-minded, Elf-loving, and adventurous than most Hobbits. He even dreams of seeing an Oliphaunt! Though clearly "bourgeois", Sam is not petty.

But Sam is "hobbity". The "lowly" that Tolkien is exalting here is not merely the physically small or the poor but the provincial, the bourgeois, the unheroic, the small-*minded* (see Ps 131). Sam is like your uncle.

God did the same sort of thing as Tolkien did over and over again in history. He used the most unpromising material. The act of creation is the supreme example, because the material there was nothing at all. Then the people He chose were more like Hobbits than like Wizards or Elves. Abraham and Sarah were old beyond childbearing, and God made their descendants as numerous as the stars. Jacob was a schemer, and God made him Israel. Joseph was the spoiled child, and God used him to save Egypt and the Jews from starvation. Moses was a stutterer, and God made him His biggest "mouth" (the literal meaning of "prophet"), who gave the world its Commandments. David was a child with sheep and a slingshot, and God made him Israel's greatest king. The twelve apostles were Hobbit-like peasants, and God made them saints. And the greatest example of all, His supreme revelation of Himself, was a tiny embryo, then a

baby born amid cow dung who grew up to become an
unemployed wanderer in a hick town and a crucified criminal. "The stone which the builders rejected has become the
head of the corner. This is the Lord's doing, and it is marvelous in our eyes" (Ps 118:22–23).

C. S. Lewis corrects a popular misunderstanding of humility when he says that to be humble is

> to take off a lot of silly, ugly, fancy-dress in which we have
> all got ourselves up and are strutting about like the little
> idiots we are. . . .
>
> Do not imagine that if you meet a really humble man
> he will be what most people call "humble" nowadays: he
> will not be a sort of greasy, smarmy person, who is always
> telling you that, of course, he is nobody. Probably all you
> will think about him is that he seemed a cheerful, intelli-
> gent chap who took a real interest in what *you* said to *him*.
> If you do dislike him it will be because you feel a little
> envious of anyone who seems to enjoy life so easily. He
> will not be thinking about humility: he will not be think-
> ing about himself at all (*Mere Christianity*, p. 114).

That is why "Humility, after the first shock, is really a
cheerful virtue" (*The Problem of Pain*, p. 67).

13.3 What should you give away?

Gift giving is a moral virtue, the actualization of charity. But
it is also a practical necessity. Many of the gifts given to the
Hobbits save their lives and save the Quest, from the mithril
coat Bilbo gave Frodo to the Phial of Galadriel, in which was
trapped the light from the Silmarils. Even a simple thing like
Sam's rope, given to him by the Elves in Lorien, twice saved
them: in descending a cliff and in capturing Gollum.

Bilbo gave up his hoard of dragon gold, and also his home and possessions to Frodo. Frodo follows the same path, giving up his life in the Shire both at the beginning, when he leaves, and at the end, when he finds that "you can't go home again". Most important of all, he gives up the Ring.

Giving the Ring away, of course, is the supreme act of giving, because the Ring is unlimited power and can get you anything you want. Only three succeed in doing this, and they are all Hobbits: Bilbo, Frodo, and Sam. Hobbits are good at giving: on their birthday they do not receive gifts but give them. Their happiness shows what Jesus says: "It is more blessed to give than to receive" (Acts 20:35). Even Gandalf's gift of fireworks, while not "serious", is symbolically appropriate because fireworks give us joy only by their "dying".

Unlike all other Quests in the world's literature, the whole point of the Ring Quest is not to *get* something (e.g., Jason's Golden Fleece, Odysseus's wife and home, Gilgamesh's immortality, or even Adam's [Milton's] Paradise Lost); but to give something up: to give this "gift" back to its maker and origin (thus destroying it), thus reversing the process of greed, materialism, idolatry, fetishism, and externalization that it symbolizes.

Frodo sacrifices not only the Ring but himself. He has no hope of surviving the journey; and when he does, he has no peace in Middle-earth. *The Lord of the Rings* ends with Frodo's "death" at the Havens—a real leave-taking, though not an ordinary biological death but a Mary-like "assumption into Heaven".

The importance of gift giving can hardly be exaggerated, especially when we realize that the greatest gifts any of us receive are the *people* who have been put into our lives for us to love.

C. S. Lewis notes that "it is much harder to receive than to give, but, I think, much more blessed." [1] For "the proper aim of giving is to put the recipient in a state where he no longer needs our gift" (*The Four Loves*, p. 76).

13.4 Does mercy trump justice?

"Pity" sometimes means a *feeling*, but when it is used in such a way as to be virtually identical with mercy (as it is in *The Lord of the Rings*), it is a *deed*.

It is mercy, not justice or courage or even heroism, that alone can defeat evil.

This is seen strikingly in the fact that at the Crack of Doom "Frodo 'failed'. . . . One must face the fact the power of Evil in the world is *not* finally resistible by incarnate creatures, however 'good'" (*Letters*, no. 191, p. 252). As Gandalf foresaw, only "the pity of Bilbo [in sparing Gollum] will rule the fate of many" (LOTR, p. 60) and save Middle-earth. Frodo's "failure" shows that pity is *necessary*:

> Regarding the failure of Frodo: Very few seem to have observed it. But following the logic of the plot, it was clearly inevitable, as an event. And surely it is a more significant and real event than a mere "fairy-story" ending in which the hero is indomitable? . . .
>
> Frodo deserved all honour because he spent every drop of his power of will and body, and that was just sufficient to bring him to the destined point, and no further. Few others, possibly no others of his time, would have got so far. The Other Power then took over: the Writer of the Story (by which I do not mean myself), "that one ever-present Person who is never absent and never named" (*Letters*, no. 192, pp. 252–53).

[1] *Letters to an American Lady* (Grand Rapids, Mich.: Eerdmans, 1967), p. 76.

Because this One is not in time, He can make something in our past as well as in our present affect the future. The salvation of Middle-earth, and of Frodo, is achieved by Frodo's (and Bilbo's, and Sam's, and Aragorn's, and Faramir's) *previous* pity and mercy to Gollum.

> That strange element in the World that we call Pity or Mercy . . . is also an absolute requirement in moral judgement since it is present in the Divine nature. . . . It must lead to the use of two different scales of "morality." To ourselves we must present the absolute ideal without compromise, for . . . if we do not aim at the highest we shall certainly fall short of the utmost that we could achieve. To others . . . we must apply a scale tempered by "mercy" . . . since we can with good will do this without the bias inevitable in judgements of ourselves (*Letters*, no. 246, p. 326).

What motivates that pity? Not mere feeling, and not utility or worldly prudence. It can seem ridiculously imprudent. But Frodo was not naïve; he knew Gollum wanted only to betray him and his promise and get the Ring back. "To pity him, to forebear to kill him, was . . . a mystical belief in the ultimate value-in-itself of pity and generosity even if disastrous in the world of time" (*Letters*, no. 192, pp. 252–53).

Jesus did the same to Judas—and with the same result.

13.5 Is charity a waste?

Why were Sauron, Isildur, and Gollum unable to resist the Ring, and why were Bilbo, Frodo, and Sam able? Part of the answer is humility, but the ultimate answer is charity (*caritas, agape*), "love" in the old sense of the word, before "love" shrunk to sex and "charity" to money. It was Frodo's love of the Shire more than himself, his willingness to give himself up for it, and Sam's love for his master:

> "I have been too deeply hurt, Sam. I tried to save the Shire, and it has been saved, but not for me. It must often be so, Sam, when things are in danger: some one has to give them up, lose them, so that others may keep them" (LOTR, p. 1006).

Amor vincit omnia: "Love (charity, self-giving, self-sacrifice) conquers all."

In a letter to his son Michael about love and marriage, Tolkien explains that self-sacrifice is not just an ideal but a necessity in this world:

> The essence of a *fallen* world is that the *best* cannot be attained by free enjoyment, or by what is called "self-realization" (usually a nice name for self-indulgence) . . . but by denial, by suffering. . . . No man, however truly he loved his betrothed and bride as a young man, has lived faithful to her as a wife in mind and body without deliberate conscious exercise of the *will*, without self-denial. Too few are told that—even those brought up "in the Church". Those outside seem seldom to have heard it (*Letters*, no. 43, pp. 51–52).

Then comes the most striking thing in all Tolkien's letters:

> Out of the darkness of my life, so much frustrated, I put before you the one great thing to love on earth: the Blessed Sacrament. . . . There you will find romance, glory, honour, fidelity, and the true way of all your loves upon earth, and more than that: Death: by the divine paradox, that which ends life, and demands the surrender of all, and yet by the taste (or foretaste) of which alone can what you seek in your earthly relationships (love,

faithfulness, joy) be maintained, or take on that complex-
ion of reality, of eternal endurance, which every man's
heart desires (*Letters*, no. 43, pp. 53–54).

C. S. Lewis writes an almost equally unforgettable passage,
on the risks and martyrdoms of charity, in *The Four Loves*:

> To love at all is to be vulnerable. Love anything, and your
> heart will certainly be wrung and possibly be broken. If
> you want to make sure of keeping it intact, you must give
> your heart to no one, not even to an animal. Wrap it
> carefully round with hobbies and little luxuries; avoid all
> entanglements; lock it up safe in the casket or coffin of
> your selfishness. But in that casket—safe, dark, motionless,
> airless—it will change. It will not be broken; it will be-
> come unbreakable, impenetrable, irredeemable. The alter-
> native to tragedy, or at least to the risk of tragedy, is
> damnation. The only place outside Heaven where you can
> be perfectly safe from all the dangers and perturbations of
> love is Hell (pp. 110–12).

Conclusion

Can any one man incarnate every truth and virtue?

Throughout the New Testament we find a shocking simplicity: Christ does not merely teach the truth, He *is* the truth; He does not merely show us the way, He *is* the way; He does not merely give us eternal life, He *is* that life. He does not merely teach or purchase our wisdom, our righteousness and sanctification and redemption, but "God made [Him] our wisdom, our righteousness and sanctification and redemption" (1 Cor 1:30). How can all these universal values and truths be really and completely present in one concrete individual person? Only if that Person is divine (thus universal) as well as human (thus particular); only by the Incarnation; only by what Lewis calls "myth become fact".

Tolkien, like most Catholics, saw pagan myths not as wholly mistaken (as most Protestants do), but as confused precursors of Christianity. Man's soul has three powers, and God left him prophets for all three: Jewish moralists for his will, Greek philosophers for his mind, and pagan mythmakers for his heart and imagination and feelings. Of course, the latter two are not infallible. C. S. Lewis calls pagan myths "gleams of celestial strength and beauty falling on a jungle of filth and imbecility" (*Perelandra*, p. 201). One of the key steps in Lewis's conversion, as recounted in his autobiography, *Surprised by Joy*, was his reading the chapter in Chesterton's *The Everlasting Man* that showed him the relationship between Christianity and pagan myths of salvation, death, and resurrection. Christianity was "myth become fact".

221

Tolkien's Catholic tradition tends to have a high opinion of pagans who know and follow the "natural law", for it interprets these pagans not apart from Christ, but as imperfectly knowing Him. For Christ is not just a thirty-three-year-old, six-foot-tall Jewish carpenter, but the eternal Logos, the Mind of God, "the true light that enlightens every man" (Jn 1:9). So Christ can be present even when not adequately known in paganism. This is exactly what St. Paul told the Athenians (in Acts 17:23): "What therefore you worship as unknown, this I proclaim to you." Christ's presence is not limited to the presence of the explicit *knowledge* of Christ, or the *revelation* of Christ. As the Reformed tradition puts it, there is also "general revelation" as well as "special revelation".

So even though *The Lord of the Rings* is not an allegory of the Gospels, we can find numerous parallels to the Gospels in *The Lord of the Rings*, since the Person at the center of the Gospels is omnipresent in hidden ways, not only in His eternal, universal nature as Truth, Goodness, and Beauty, but even in His particular historical manifestation, His Incarnation. For instance, Frodo's journey up Mount Doom is strikingly similar to Christ's Way of the Cross. Sam is his Simon of Cyrene, but he carries the cross bearer as well as the cross.

There is no one complete, concrete, visible Christ figure in *The Lord of the Rings*, like Aslan in Narnia. But Christ is really, though invisibly, present in the whole of *The Lord of the Rings*. *The Lord of the Rings* is like the Eucharist. Under its appearances we find Christ, who under these (pagan, universal) figures (symbols, not allegories), is truly hidden: *quae sub his figuris vere latitat.*

He is more clearly present in Gandalf, Frodo, and Aragorn, the three Christ figures. First of all, all three undergo different forms of death and resurrection (see section 5.1).

Second, all three are saviors: through their self-sacrifice they help save all of Middle-earth from the demonic sway of Sauron. Third, they exemplify the Old Testament threefold Messianic symbolism of prophet (Gandalf), priest (Frodo), and king (Aragorn). These three "job descriptions" correspond to the three distinctively human powers of the soul, as discovered by nearly every psychologist from Plato to Freud: head, heart, and hands, or mind, emotions, and will. For this reason many great tales have three protagonists: Gandalf, Frodo, and Aragorn; Mr. Spock, Bones McCoy, and Captain Kirk; Ivan, Alyosha, and Dmitri Karamazov; St. John the philosophical mystic, St. James the practical moralist, and St. Peter the courageous leader and Rock.

A fourth hidden presence of Christ in *The Lord of the Rings* is in the theme of divine providence (see section 2.2); for from the New Testament point of view Christ is the supreme example in history of divine providence—in fact, the single point of all other examples, of all history.

A fifth presence of Christ in *The Lord of the Rings* is in the creative power of its language (see sections 9.1 and 9.3). Christ is the Logos, the Word of God. He is mentioned in the Bible as early as Genesis 1:3 (cf. Jn 1:3), but as a verb, not a noun.

A sixth presence is ecclesial. Tolkien was a Catholic and called *The Lord of the Rings* "a Catholic book" (see section 2.4). He removed "churches" from *The Lord of the Rings* not only to avoid anachronism but also to show the presence, in the depths of his plot, of the universal ("catholic") Church. For the Church is not only an organization but also an organism, an invisible, "mystical" Body, a "fellowship". The word "church", from the Greek *ek-klesia*, means "the called-out". A good description of the Fellowship of the Ring.

For the Church, too, is a "fellowship of a ring", but her

ring is exactly the opposite of Sauron's. It is the Eucharist: a little wafer that is equally round, but full rather than empty; the humble extension of the Incarnation of God into man rather than the proud self-exaltation of man in order to make himself God. The Ring takes your life, your blood, like Dracula, a perfect opposite to Christ, Who comes to give His blood, to give us a blood transfusion. The two symbols are perfect opposites: the Ring of Power and the Bread of Weakness, the Lord of the Rings and the Lamb of God.

The whole of history, as revealed in the Bible, is the cosmic *jihad* between Christ and Antichrist, martyr and vampire, humility of God versus pride of man. Throughout the Bible there is vertical symbolism exemplifying this contrast. Paradise is made in Eden by God's self-giving descent and lost through man's self-taking, man's succumbing to the devil's temptation to become "like God". The apparent rise is really the "fall". After Paradise is lost, the City of Man tries to rise up to Heaven again by its own power, in the Tower of Babel, and falls. And when Paradise is finally regained, the New Jerusalem of the City of God descends from Heaven as a grace.

The most fundamental Christian symbol is the Cross. This also is perfectly opposite to the Ring. The Cross gives life; the Ring takes it. The Cross gives you death, not power; the Ring gives you power even over death. The Ring squeezes everything into its inner emptiness; the Cross expands in all four directions, gives itself to the emptiness, filling it with its blood, its life. The Ring is Dracula's tooth. The Cross is God's sword, held at the hilt by the hand of Heaven and plunged into the world not to take our blood but to give us His. The Cross is Christ's hypodermic; the Ring is Dracula's bite. The Cross saves other wills; the Ring dominates other wills. The Cross liberates; the Ring enslaves.

The Cross works only freely, by the vulnerability of love. Love is vulnerable to rejection, and thus apparent failure. Frodo offers Gollum free kindness, but he fails to win Gollum's trust and fails himself, at the Crack of Doom, to complete his task. But his philosophy does not fail.

He could have used the philosophy of Sauron, of the Ring. He could have used force and compelled Gollum, or even justly killed him. But no one can make another person good by controlling his will, not even God. Frodo nearly won Gollum by his kindness, but Gollum chose not to trust and lost both his body and his soul. Frodo failed.

There is no room for failure in the philosophy of Sauron. There is room for failure in the philosophy of Tolkien, for the philosophy of Tolkien is simply Christianity. And according to Christianity, the most revealing thing that ever happened in history happened at another Crack of Doom, when Christ "failed", lost, died. That was how the meek little Lamb defeated the great dragon beast (see Rev 17, especially verse 14): by His blood. Frodo did what Christ did, and it "worked" because Christ did it, because it was real, not fantasy, and it was real because the real world is a "Christian" world. Only in a Christian world can this "failure" have such power.

It is a very strange philosophy. A few pagan sages like Lao Tzu understood the principle of the power of weakness, but he did not know it would come from a literal, bloody event in history. Neither did Frodo. Like Socrates, Buddha, and Lao Tzu, Frodo did not see Christ, yet somehow believed: "Blessed are those who have not seen and yet believe" (Jn 20:29).

BIBLIOGRAPHY

Bruner, Kurt, and Jim Ware. *Finding God in The Lord of the Rings.* Wheaton, Ill: Tyndale House, 2001.

Caldecott, Stratford. "The Horns of Hope". *Chesterton Review.* Vol. 28, nos. 1 and 2. Feb./May 2002.

———. *Secret Fire: The Spiritual Vision of JRR Tolkien.* London: Darton, Longman and Todd, 2005. American edition: *The Power of the Ring: The Spiritual Vision behind The Lord of the Rings.* New York: Crossroad Publishing Co., 2005.

Lewis, C. S. *The Abolition of Man or Reflections on Education with Special Reference to the Teaching of English in the Upper Form Schools.* New York: Macmillan, 1947, 1955.

———. *The Allegory of Love.* New York: Oxford University Press, 1958.

———. *The Four Loves.* London: Collins Fontana, 1960.

———. *God in the Dock: Essays on Theology and Ethics.* Edited by Walter Hooper. Grand Rapids, Mich.: W. B. Eerdmans, 1970.

———. *The Last Battle.* New York: Macmillan, 1956.

———. *Letters to Children.* New York: Macmillan, 1985.

———. *Letters to Malcolm.* New York: Harcourt, Brace and World, 1963.

———. *The Magician's Nephew.* New York: Macmillan, 1970.

———. *Mere Christianity.* New York: Macmillan Publishing Co, Inc., 1943, 1945, 1952.

———. *Miracles: A Preliminary Study.* New York: Macmillan Publishing Co., Inc., 1947, 1960.

———. *Out of the Silent Planet.* New York: Macmillan, 1965.

———. *Perelandra.* New York: Macmillan, 1944.

———. *The Pilgrim's Regress: An Allegorical Apology for Christianity*. Grand Rapids, Mich.: W. B. Eerdman's, 1981.

———. *The Problem of Pain*. New York: Macmillan, 1978.

———. *The Screwtape Letters*. New York: Macmillan, 1957.

———. *Selected Literary Essays*. Edited by Walter Hooper. Cambridge, Eng.: Cambridge University Press, 1969.

———. *That Hideous Strength*. New York: Macmillan, 1965.

———. *Till We Have Faces*. New York: Harcourt, Brace, 1956.

———. *The Weight of Glory and Other Addresses*. Rev. ed. New York: Macmillan, 1980.

———. *The World's Last Night and Other Essays*. New York: Harcourt, Brace, Jovanovitch, 1952, 1960.

Lewis, C. S., ed. *George MacDonald: An Anthology*. New York: Macmillan, 1978.

Picard, Max. *The World of Silence*. Chicago: Regnery, 1952.

Purtill, Richard L. *J. R. R. Tolkien: Myth, Morality and Religion*. San Francisco: Ignatius Press, 2003.

Shippey, Tom. *J. R. R. Tolkien: Author of the Century*. Boston: Houghton Mifflin, 2002.

Tolkien, J. R. R. *The Letters of J. R. R. Tolkien*. Edited by Humphrey Carpenter, with the assistance of Christopher Tolkien. Boston: Houghton Mifflin, 1981; © 1981 by George Allen & Unwin, Ltd.

———. *The Lord of the Rings*. Boston: Houghton Mifflin, 1987, 1994.

———. *The Silmarillion*. Edited by Christopher Tolkien. Boston: Houghton Mifflin, 1977.

———. *The Tolkien Reader*. New York: Ballantine Books, 1966. (This book contains "On Fairy-Stories".)

Vanauken, Sheldon. *A Severe Mercy*. San Francisco: Harper and Row, 1977.

APPENDIX

A CONCORDANCE
References for the philosophy of Tolkien

KEY: page numbers that are preceded by:

— no letter refer to *The Lord of the Rings* (Boston: Houghton Mifflin, 1994)
— the letter S refer to *The Silmarillion* (Boston: Houghton Mifflin, 1977)
— the letters FS refer to "On Fairy-Stories" in *The Tolkien Reader* (New York: Ballantine Books, 1966)
— the letter L refer to *The Letters of J. R. R. Tolkien* (Boston: Houghton Mifflin, 1981)

Pages are divided into five parts, so that, e.g., 3a refers to the top 20 percent of page 3, and 7d to the fourth 20 percent of page 7, etc. When two letters are given (e.g., 5de), they may refer to 40 percent of page five or to a short passage on the border of 5d and 5e.

The themes are outlined by number. Bold type indicates the more important passages:

1. Metaphysics
1.1. *Metaphysical realism: that reality is more than appearance, more than our consciousness, and more than our expectations*
2d, 43c, 115a, 169d, 203a, 205d, 214c, 219d, 220d, 221d, 271a, 307d, 319d, 364e, 453a, 498b, 633b, 646e, 647c, 652c, **FS33c**, FS64ab, FS77, L145a, L231cd, L239c

1.2. *Supernaturalism: that reality is more than the natural (matter, time, and space)*
190e, 204c, 216e, 217a, 218b, 225b, 229c, 491a–c, 595d, 901c, FS38a, FS49d–50b, FS51d, FS52a, FS56d

1.3. *Platonism: archetypes*
27cde, 35c, 57a, 72cde, 81ab, 108bc, 122c, 129b, 139c, 219a, 221c, 228bcd, 229c, 234e, 258e, 289b, 305b–e, 309d, 314d, 315c, 323c, 340c, 341e, 342ab, 452cd, 460b, 490cd, 491bc, 501c, 513c, 528c, 529e, 541d, 591a, 613c–614c, 703d, 704cd, 707c–e, 709bc, 734c, 736e, 738a, 768e, 780e, 810b, 811b, 813e, 823a, 898e, 899e, 916e, 941d, 950c, 951a, 964c, L347ab

2. Philosophical Theology

2.1. *God*
116d, 122c, 139a, 261b, **351e**, 471e, S20b, FS51d, **L234d, L253c, L413cde**

2.2. *Divine providence (especially providential timings and "coincidences")*
54d–55a, 60a, 68d, 74d, 77c, 116cd, 123e, 165e, 236a, 247b, 310a, 394e, 397de, 484e, **485c**, **486cd**, 489c, 581a, 604e–605a, 612b, 613a, 644b, 653d, 695c, 699a–d, 763, 797bc, 811c, 814c, 816d, 826d, 841e, 859d, 861c, 921b, **926d**, 957cd

2.3. *Fate (or predestination, or destiny) and free will*
11b,d, 58d, 60a, **263e–264b**, 359c, 367bc, 392bc, **423e**, 474b, 505cd, 580c, 590a, **626a**, 666a, 671a, 691d, 715c, 756c, 762b, 764bc, 766c, 780cd, 786c, 797d, 829e, 855c, 861b, 891b, 923a, 926c, 928a

2.4. *Religion*
232b, 323a, 323c, **661bc**, 934b, FS51c, **FS88c–90a**, **L172c, L201d, L220ab, L243e, L283e**

3. Angelology

3.1. *The reality of angels*
169d, 216e–217a, 355de, 491b–d, 505a, 556a, 579e,
704c, 740de, 741e, 742cd, 946e, 950a, 996e–997a, S15a,
S18d, S20c, S21cd, S25d, S26c, L202abc, L159e

3.2. *The task of angels: guardians*
5c, 25a, 242c, 491b, 549b, 742a, 757e–758a, 759cd,
762e, 852c, 930a, 971b, 974a, L99abc

3.3. *Elves as halfway between the human and the angelic*
77cd, 78c, 85c, 219d, 231a, 355e, 364b, 367c, 368e,
369d, 379b–e, 432b, 454b, 457de, 597d, 664a–c, 712d,
963ab, S26b,d, FS38c, FS72d, FS73e, FS85c, L176c,
L185c, L145c

4. Cosmology

4.1. *The beauty of the cosmos*
27c–e, 127e, 339e, 341e, 342bc, 352a, 453cd, 458a,
462c, 462e–463a, 471e, 534b, 535a, 541cd, 597d, 633b,
815a, 852c, 899de, 956d, S18b, FS33bc, FS38b, FS78de,
L177c, L280d

4.2. *The personality of things in the world*
54c, 108bc, 116b, 128a, 172d, 173a, 179d, 209c 281e,
282a, 285c, 321e, 448e, 450de, 452cd, 453b, 488b, 516e,
528c, 731e, 954c, FS78de

4.3. *Magic in the world and man*
209cd, 218c, 232a, 248ab, 251b, 255bc, 267a, 273a,
276d, 281c,e, 282a, 285c, 327e, 330ab, 351e, 353a,
361bc, 367c, 431c, 457a, 539cd, 553a, 608c, 615c, 679d,
692a, 705e–706a, 713a, 768e, 783e, 789d, 790d, 810e,
819d, 826d, 827b, 849e, 858b, 866c, 880d, 882a–c,
898bc, 902a, 914c, 915b, FS38a–39c (in the cosmos);
171a, 185d, 193e, 227c, 306d, 491c, 635a, 757e–758a,

863d, 927d, 956c, FS39bc, FS73e, FS74d, L200b (in man)

5. Anthropology

5.1. *Death*

64c, 139c, 140a, 189e, 271c–e, 289b, 340a, 405ab, **484c**, 485c, 490c, 613c–614c, 662e, 715b, 764a, 780e, 785e, 807a, 836a, 842a, 874d, 935de, 952e, 965c–966d, 1006a, 1007c, FS85c, **L246c, L267c,** L286b

5.2. *Romance*

464de, 504b, 767c–e, 849c, 938d, 939d, 941c–e, 943c–e, 951d, 953c, 955de, **L48–54a,** L161a, L229d, L230a

5.3. *The perilous status of selfhood; the flexibility of the self*

46c, 213e, 217c, 423cd, 504d, 505e, 506c, 511d, 528a, 569d, 602c, 604cd, 618d–619d, 626cd, **629c,** 638c, 761c, 792d, 856e, **870c,** 926bc, 934e, 947a, 952e, 961e, 1006a

5.4. Sehnsucht, *longing (especially for the sea)*

35a,c, 41e, 42bc, 44c, 62c, 76de, 78c, 80a, 342b, 369a,b,d, 464b, 933c, 1005c, FS41c, FS56cd, **FS63c–64c,** FS74a, FS84bc, FS86a–c, FS87ab (in general); 7a, 44b, 106d, 339d, 342c, 617e, 827b, **855de,** 857e, 935d, 964cd, 1007de, **S19ab,e, S26e–27a,** S30d, L347ab (on the sea)

6. Epistemology

6.1. *Knowledge is not always good*

33a, 47b, 51e–52a, 53b, 54b, 82b, 216bc, 252d, 258c, 264a, 269b, 279ab, 391–392c, **448b, 583c,** 591a, 696c–e, 748c, 762e, **838d,** 918b–d, FS33c, L174d, L333d

6.2. *Knowledge by intuition*

46e, 58d, 73c, 116c, 168c, 172a, 185d, 195b, 207b, 244e, 251e, 254e, 301d, 336c, 375b, 388b–d, 394b–d, 457d,

479e, 533de, 581d, 652ab, 653c, 657d, 682c, 691c, 718c, 723c, 921b, 941de, 942a

6.3. *Knowledge by faith (trust)*
103c, 115a, 167a, 179d, 262d, **300b–d**, 388d, 424e, 485e, 564b, 565bc, 566e, 568d, 626d, 629c, 666a, 672e, 673c, 743a, 796b, 958c, 995d

6.4. *Truth*
601d–602b, 603d, 607e, 618de, FS42bc, FS63c, FS74e–75c, **FS87d–90a**, L194c

7. Philosophy of History

7.1. *Teleology, story, purpose, "road"*
xvac, 1b, 2e, 35c, 65a, 72c–e, 76c,e, 83b, 85e, 104ab, 226a, 236ab, 264a, 354ab, 463b, 484b, 504a, 590a, 632a, 679c, **696b–697a**, 714c, 715c,e, 748e, 756c, 758c, 762c, 918a, 920d, 928b, 929e, 936d, 949e, 954e, 957e, 965e, 974e, 997c, 1006d, 1008b, L239de

7.2. *Tradition, collective memory, legends*
7cd, 9c, 43c, 78c, 146c, 155–156, 186d, 187b, 196de, 200de, 201c, 236b, 241b, 271c,e, 364e, 365b, 369d, 423d, 424c, 425b, 431e, 452e, 458cd, 500b, 513e, 528c, 531a, 537a, 544d, 545d, 583b, 632e, 696e–697a, 706d, 707c–e, 764bc, 847b, 946d, 950cd, 956c, 1006c, L185c, L333d, FS56b

7.3. *The freedom and unpredictability of history*
50bc, 72d, 104b, 105c, 260c, **264ab**, 274ab, 626a, 665c, 696e, 924d, 950e, 957e, S15c, S18a, L91e, L160b

7.4. *Devolution, pessimism*
51b, 129b, 142e, 181b, 186e, 215a, 223c, 238a, 262bc, 300d, 308a, 309a, **340c**, 368e, 369ab, 383de, 457a, 463d, 464b, 511a, 646e, 647a, 655c, 662de, 646e, 663e, 664b, 742e, 804b, 806b, 813bc, 842a, **855a–c**, 949e–950a, 953c, 956a, 981a, 993c, FS56b, FS79c, FS81b, FS81e–82a, FS83a, FS83c

10. Political Philosophy

10.1. *Populism, "small is beautiful"*
xviid, 1cd, 9c–e, 10a, 226bc, 946de, 975e, 977b,d, 983e,
L63d–64a, L246

10.2. *Peace and war*
5c–e, 58cd, 506c, 513e, 523e, 524b, 566c, **600d–601b**,
646d, 650c, **656e**, 820c, 860c–e, 862a–c, 937de, 983c,
986e–987a, 992c–e, 993a, 996e, L178e–179a

11. Ethics

11.1. *Spiritual warfare*
154d, 157d, 165de, 194a, 339bc, 343a, 348b, **392bc**,
417e, 505c, 542b, 564e, 565bc, 602b, 616d, 618d–619d,
662e, 748e, 832e, 833c, 838e, 862a–c, 922de, 994d,
S16b,e, **L197b–d**, L221d

11.2. *The power of evil and the evil of power*
46a, **50b**, 59d, 162d, 189c, 239c, 332b, 355b, **489b**,
490d, 515a, **537b**, 564b, 616d, 632a, 677, 680c, 691b,
702a, 704d, 804e, 810, 811, 832e, 833c, 838c–e, 860c–e,
861ab, 864b, 880d, 916e, 924cd, 967b, 970d, 994d,
L252c,e

11.3. *The weakness of evil*
170e, 254c, **261b**, 343a, 474e, 485e–486b, 509a, 568a,
571a, 581a, 687bc, 705c, 713a, 797e, 816d, 858c, 860e,
861a, 862a, 879a, 890c, 893a, **901bc**, 924e, 926d, 928c,
996b, S17c, L76b, L243c, L337c

11.4. *The strategy of evil; the mechanism of temptation
(especially the Ring)*
33cd, 45e, 54bc, 59c, 235a–c, 237b–d, 248b, 252cd,
261a, 309d, 349a, 356de, 357c, 388–390, 550a, 570d–
571a, **583c**, 656d, 691d, 795de, 836a, 838c, 880e, 890e–
891a, 921de, 922de, 924cd, 925c, 961a–c, S31c, L88a,
L94a, **L145e–146a**, L200b, **L279e**

12. Ethics: The Hard Virtues

1. *Duty versus utility*

60a, 85e, 235e, 262d, 274b, 349a, 356ab, 409c, **427e–428a**, 430c, 475c, 507a, 600d–601b, 610c, 623d, 672a, 692e, 711b, 714c, 716d, 718cd, 724b, 756c, 766e, 767a, 829a, 834e, 861b, 862c, 903a, 913a, 918bc, 923c

12.2. *Courage*

83c, 137–138, 504d, **507a**, 553b, 695d, 696c, 711b, 715b, 717e, 719c, 823d, 863d, 868cd, 913b, 914e

12.3. *Hope versus despair*

262c–e, 324a, 505d, **624ab**, 653a, 692c,e, 714ab, 723c, 749, 755c, 758c, 783c, 797a, 807a, 819d, 826b, 834c, 835a, 835cd, 859d, 862c, 871, 873d, 874de, 887c, 890d, **912e–913c**, 918, 923b, 929

12.4. *Obedience to authority*

389b, 390bc, 510d, 569b–d, 580c, 624a, 677d, 715c, 763bc, 766c, 767b, 809c, 835a, 836b, 837a, 870e, 922e, 979c,d, 982, **L202d**, L243e

12.5. *Honesty, truthfulness, keeping promises*

11e–12a, 584d, **603d–604d**, 610a, 626a,c, 629c, 649d, 654b, 665e–666a, 672e–673a, 674d, 767b, 786b, 818c, 851c, 858e

13. Ethics: The Soft Virtues

13.1. *Friendship, fellowship*

61e, 85b, 102ab, 103c, 235e–236a, 245b, 269c, 300d, 334d, 338c–339c, 347c, 348b, 394bc, 397, 409cd, 485a, 714e, 718cd, 724b, 881a, 889c, **919de**, 926d, 929b

13.2. *Humility, "hobbitry"*

262e, 356c, 357a, 389bc, 570de, 852a, **852c**, FS66a, **L64a** (humility); 1cd, 2bc, 7d, 47e, 76a, 99c, 100b, 137bc, 226bc, **264a**, **543a–c**, 544e–545a, 560c, 630b,

692c, 739c, **811c**, L145c, L158e, L160bc, L232a, L244e, L245e, L288e ("hobbitry")

13.3. *Gifts*

2c, 5e, 203c, 270c,d, 310a, 327c, 360c,e, 510e, 679d, 704b, 712d, 758c, 891d, 956a–c, 964e, 999d

13.4. *Pity*

58b, 509c, 570d, **600d–601b**, 670e, 699a–d, 923bc, 926d, 961ab, 983a, 995e, **L253ab**, **L326a–c**

13.5. *Charity, the gift of self*

61b, 237b–d, 260d, 475c, 743a, 760d, **862bc**, 917e, 931de, 965a–c, **1006bc**, L202de, L246ab, L253b, L327b

14. The Fulfillment of All the Points: Christ

260d, 322ab, 346e, 389e, 484ab, 655d, 742a, 749d, 762ab, 829b, 842d, 844e, 848a, 850e, 856c, 857a, 858b,e, 862bc, 870e, 915ab, 917e, 918cd, 919de, 931cd, 935b, 936d, 937cd, 945e, 947a,d, 948ab, 1002c,d, **1006a–c**